EXPLORE

Z for Zachariah

ROBERT O'BRIEN

Guide written by
Claire Wright

Series Editor: Stewart Martin

A **Letts** Literature Guide

Extracts from *Z for Zachariah* by Robert O'Brien are reprinted by kind permission of Victor Gollancz

First published 1995

Letts Educational
Aldine House
Aldine Place
London W12 8AW

Text © Claire Wright 1995

Typeset by Jordan Publishing Design

Text Design Jonathan Barnard

Cover and text illustrations Hugh Marshall

Graphic illustration Hugh Marshall

Design © BPP (Letts Educational) Ltd

British Library Cataloguing in Publication Data

A CIP record for this book is available from the British Library

ISBN 1 85758 274 8

Printed and bound in Great Britain by Ashford Colour Press Ltd, Gosport, Hants.

Letts Educational is the trading name of BPP (Letts Educational) Ltd

Contents

◼ Plot synopsis

Fifteen-year-old Ann Burden lives alone on her family's farm in Burden Valley, in the USA. There has been a nuclear war: the high-walled valley was sheltered from the radiation, but everything outside is dead. Ann's family went out to look for survivors and never came back. For a whole year, Ann has believed that she is the only person left alive in the world, and has organised herself to survive alone. But now she sees a column of smoke, getting closer. Ann is excited, but also afraid to think someone is coming, and decides not to show herself at first. She destroys all signs of her presence, and camps in a hidden cave overlooking the house. A man arrives in a strange plastic suit, and Ann watches unseen as he joyfully discovers the valley and farm.

The stranger explores and finds the pond, with its living fish. Hot and tired, he bathes in Burden Creek – unaware that it is not the same stream that flows into the pond: the creek comes from outside the valley, and is poisoned. Faro (Ann's cousin's dog) turns up and befriends the stranger. From her hiding place, Ann sees the man grow ill, and when he fails to emerge from his tent, she is desperately worried. Although she still knows nothing about the man, she realises how much she wants company again. She goes to the tent and finds him very ill: he tells her it is radiation sickness, and he will get worse before he gets better. Ann moves the man into the house and nurses him as best she can. She learns that he is John Loomis, a chemist who helped to invent the radiation-proof plastic suit. He survived the war because he was in his sheltered laboratory, with provisions – and the first prototype of the plastic suit – when the bombing began.

For a while, Loomis seems better, though very weak. He makes practical suggestions about the farm. Ann enjoys his company and likes helping him: she even starts thinking innocently that they might get married.

Suddenly, Loomis grows worse again. He has feverish nightmares about someone called Edward, and about the plastic suit being stolen. Ann finally pieces the story together. Edward was with Loomis in the lab, and when he tried to take the suit to find his family outside, Loomis had to shoot him to stop him. Ann is disturbed by this knowledge, but still prays desperately that Loomis will not die.

Loomis recovers from the brink of death, nursed devotedly by Ann, despite her new doubts about him. At first he is simply grateful, but as he grows stronger, the balance of their relationship changes. Knowing now that he will live, Loomis begins to plan obsessively for the future. He starts to make decisions about the farm. Ann grows uneasy. She tries to find out more about Loomis, but when she innocently asks if he was married, he takes it as a 'come-on', and grabs her. Ann senses that he is trying to take possession of her, like everything else. Loomis' behaviour grows more and more intimidating, until one night he tries to rape Ann. She escapes, horrified, to her cave.

Loomis is still weak, so Ann continues to work the farm and leave him food. She will not let him die – but she cannot trust him now, either. She disguises her route to and from the cave each day, but knows that Loomis is trying to find her hiding place. Soon, he is independent of her help. He takes the tractor keys, and locks up the store. Is he paranoid about conserving resources, or trying to force Ann back to him? When Ann confronts him, he shoots her in the ankle: she realises that he actually intends to imprison her. Loomis hunts Ann, using Faro to track her down. He destroys her camp, and for a month, she is a desperate fugitive in the hills. Her worst fears of the stranger have come true. Ann dreams of a place outside the valley, and resolves to steal the suit and try to find it. When Faro is killed following her across the poisoned creek, she is ready to leave.

She tricks Loomis away from the house and takes the suit. At the edge of the deadness, she waits for him to come after her. Determined though she is, she cannot shoot Loomis, and expects him to kill her, like Edward, for the suit. But when she challenges him, he breaks down, and lets her go. At the last moment, he points her in the right direction. Leaving him wretchedly alone in the valley, Ann walks into the deadness. With hope.

Echoes of Eden

'A for Adam... Z for Zachariah'

'Since I knew that Adam was the first man, for a long time I assumed that Zachariah must be the last man.'

Adam and Eve were the first (and only) two people in a world newly created. Loomis and Ann may be the last (and only) two people in a world otherwise destroyed.

A need for companionship...

' "It is not good for the man to be alone. I will make a helper suitable for him." ' (Genesis 2:18)

... suddenly fulfilled.

'While he was sleeping... he brought her to the man.' (Genesis 2:21–22)

An ideal partnership...

'The man and his wife were both naked, and they felt no shame.' (Genesis 2:25)

... shaken by the temptation of power an the end of innocence...

' "When you eat of it your eyes will be opened, and you will be like God, knowing good and evil." ' (Genesis 3:

green place...

And the LORD God made all kinds of... trees that were pleasing to the eye and good for food.' (Genesis 2:8–9)

... and a simple life.

'The LORD God... put him in the Garden of Eden to work it and take care of it.' (Genesis 2:15)

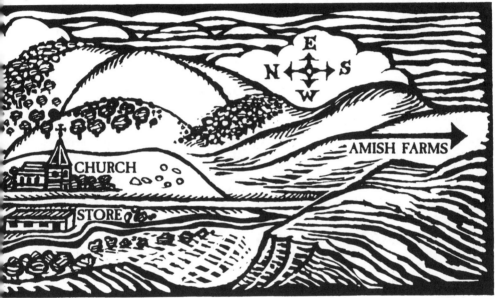

CHURCH

STORE

AMISH FARMS

.. and ruined.

I was afraid... so I hid.'
(Genesis 3:10)

A secret too dangerous to keep

'He must not be allowed to ... take also from the tree of life and eat, and live for ever.' (Genesis 3:22)

Exile to an unknown world

'So the LORD God banished him from the Garden of Eden.' (Genesis 3:23)

Ann Burden

Ann has been brought up on an isolated farm in rural America, going to school in Ogdentown (25 miles away). As the novel opens, she is a month short of her sixteenth birthday. Because the story is told as Ann's diary, and she seldom thinks about her appearance, we know only that she is skinny, with straight-cropped hair and boyish clothes. However, her personal diary gives us a full and clear insight into her thoughts and feelings. Robert O'Brien uses the extreme nature of Ann's situation to explore aspects of character rarely called upon in everyday life.

Ann is a survivor. Her farm upbringing has equipped her with tremendous common sense, practicality and resourcefulness. She is at home in nature, and is able to use the land, plants and animals to feed herself. She can fish, shoot, drive a tractor, work machinery and cook: she even makes a competent nurse. She is good at thinking methodically through problems, at planning ahead and organising things. She is also sensible and cautious about possible dangers – like Burden Creek, or the approaching stranger.

Ann has not fallen apart on her own, but has established routines and work for herself: she is quite independent and self-contained. When the stranger appears, she controls her excitement: she is realistic enough to know that not all people are kind or trustworthy (especially in a struggle to survive). She is brave and determined, and does not give way to self-pity – despite the loss of her family and everything she has known. She faces up to problems, enjoys hard work and looks to the future instead of the past: this tough hopefulness is a key note of Ann's character.

On its own, all this might make Ann seem too good to be true, even rather a cold character. But she also experiences loss, fear, uncertainty, anger, even desperation at times: she is very honest about these feelings in her diary. She does not allow herself to think about her family, because she needs all her hope and courage for the future, but we sense the deep-down loneliness and grief when she dreams, at moments of stress, that her family has returned. For all her resilience, Ann is sensitive and vulnerable: Loomis' cruelty and ingratitude hurt her deeply. And for all her independence, Ann is a 'people person'. She is compassionate, tolerant and friendly. She loves to be useful, whether as a nurse or (as she still hopes) a teacher.

Moreover, Ann's practical competence is balanced by a rich imaginative and spiritual side. Her mind has been nourished by reading the Bible, poetry and 'any good writing': books are essential for her to live to the full. She has a deeply religious nature, often visiting the little church to pray. She plays the piano, especially enjoying hymns. These aspects of her life are very important to Ann, and she tries – in vain – to share them with Loomis. They give her strength, hope and pleasure; an appreciation of beauty and an imaginative sympathy for other people. Ann also has a strong, old-fashioned sense of morality. She values human life (she would finally rather die than kill) and is fair and dutiful towards Loomis – even after he attacks her. She is also very innocent, dreaming with moving simplicity of a church wedding to Loomis.

In all, Ann is a very rounded character. Her balance of outer competence and inner resources, of strength and sensitivity, allows her not just to survive, but to find pleasure and purpose in life. Like the clear stream, she has her source in the natural, sheltered world of the valley: and like it, she remains pure and full of life, despite the poison and death of the outside world.

John Loomis

John Loomis

All we know of Loomis is what Ann can learn from his words and actions. She can only guess at his feelings, thoughts and intentions – and there is no all-knowing 'outside' narrator to explain them. This makes us identify more closely with Ann, and also creates suspense, as Loomis' history and character are revealed bit by bit.

Loomis is in his early thirties, pale and thin. With his long dark hair and beard, he looks wild and 'rather poetic': when they are trimmed Ann thinks he looks 'quite nice' and 'almost handsome'. He tells her that he was a chemist for the Navy, and went on to do research at Cornell University, where he was recruited for a secret government project. He spent three years in an underground laboratory, developing a new type of radiation-proof plastic. Loomis was (he says) alone in the lab, with the only prototype of a radiation-proof suit, when the war started. (Later, from his haunted dreams, we find out that there was someone else, called Edward, with him and that Loomis shot him dead to stop him taking the suit.) Months later, Loomis ventured out in search of survivors, and finally found Burden Valley.

When we first see Loomis, he is cautious and methodical, a bit like Ann. He also shows hints of humanity which draw Ann to him: excitement briefly overcomes his caution, when he jumps into the stream. When he falls ill, he is calm and realistic. He is grateful for Ann's care, and tries to make helpful suggestions about the farming. He shows a touching enjoyment of simple pleasures. It seems that after all Ann has nothing to fear from the stranger.

However, Ann becomes increasingly uneasy at Loomis' nightmares about Edward, and his paranoia about the suit. She finally learns that he is a 'murderer' – but what were his motives? Perhaps he *had* to kill Edward, not just to save himself, but to protect the suit for the human race. In Loomis' dreams, we glimpse terrible guilt and fear, which he suppresses when he is conscious. Loomis has experienced at first hand the desperate struggle for survival, the death and devastation of the war. Unlike Ann, he lacks the inner resources to deal with his trauma. He is not close to the land, which gives Ann both physical and emotional nourishment. He is a scientist, with none of Ann's imagination or sensitivity: he is interested in technical books, not literature, and regards Ann's prayers as a waste of time. He also lacks her moral decency: he has already killed to achieve his purposes.

Once Loomis knows that he will survive, he begins to make plans: he wants to establish 'a colony, one that will last permanently'. But the war has taught him fear and mistrust: he develops an obsessive need to have everything under his control. He works secretively to become independent of Ann, and gathers knowledge so that he can take over the farming. Ann is happy to share, but Loomis needs to control – not just the valley, but Ann herself. He pursues her with cold, ruthless cunning, and, ironically, drives her to do exactly what he most fears: steal the suit.

Loomis finds that with Ann – just as with Edward – he has gained control, but lost his only friend in the process. When Ann reminds him of this, he finally shows his deep fear of being left alone. Perhaps he also faces up to what he has done: his last impulse, pointing Ann towards signs of life, is generous.

Robert O'Brien invites us to compare Ann and Loomis, and how they handle their extraordinary circumstances. Unlike Ann, Loomis puts theory and logic above emotions and the needs of other people: he plans for survival coldly, without Ann's hopes and dreams. Although both of them have learned to fear and distrust strangers, Loomis carries his suspicions to extremes: unlike Ann, he lacks the inner resources to stay human in the face of war. Like Burden Creek, he has been contaminated by its poison, and brings it with him into the valley.

Faro (the dog)

Faro belonged to Ann's cousin David. Ann thought he had left the valley to look for David and died, but he turns up again when Loomis arrives. Faro's relationship to Loomis in many ways mirrors Ann's. He too is cautious at first, but has no choice but to risk trusting the stranger. He too has survived on his own, but is naturally friendly. He too 'adopts' Loomis and for a while flourishes happily. He shares Ann's pleasure in outdoor life, and even the church. When Loomis takes control, he imprisons Faro and uses him for his own purposes – just as he tries to do with Ann.

Faro's efficient tracking faces Ann with a dilemma just like Loomis' with Edward: will she shoot Faro – her only friend – to save herself?

The dead

Z for Zachariah sets up a situation where there may be only two people left in the world. This makes us (and Ann) intensely aware of all the other people who have *not* survived. There is Ann's family, the Kleins who owned the store, the people in Ogdentown, the Amish farmers, the man Ann heard on the radio, the people Loomis found at the Air Force base: all now dead.

There is also Edward, whose memory haunts Loomis in his fever. For Ann, Edward is a distinct person: she feels sorry for him, trapped in the lab knowing his wife and son were outside. In many ways, he was like Ann. He held on passionately to a 'wild hope', and so posed a threat to Loomis' cold, logical plans. Having sensibly asked just to borrow the suit, he had to steal it, and finally faced Loomis and his gun – as Ann does.

Only Ann has the imagination to dream of *living* people. They call her out of the valley, with hope.

Themes and images in *Z for Zachariah*

The valley

The valley

Ann writes in detail about the geography of Burden Valley, giving directions and distances: it is a realistic place. But the valley is also a simplified setting. The high surrounding hills help to explain the valley's survival, but they also make it a special environment, cut off from the world. They form the boundary between a symbolic 'inside' and 'outside': inside is nature and peace, while outside is deadness and war. The valley has two streams – one from inside, and one from outside. They too are symbolic: will Loomis 'contaminate' Ann with the 'poison' he brings in from outside, as Burden Creek does when it meets the clear stream?

The valley contains only what is essential for human life. Nature provides water, food (plant and animal) and shelter. It also offers beauty, for those, like Ann, who can see it. The store fulfils Ann's physical needs – for food, clothing and other basics – and helps us to believe that she could have survived as she has. The church fulfils her spiritual needs. The house is an emotional anchor: it represents home and family to Ann.

The valley is like an island on which the characters are marooned. They are cut off from normal life and have to be resourceful – even competitive – to survive. There are no rules or routines, unless they choose to make them. They cannot run away from problems, or each other: there is nowhere to go.

The valley is also like the garden of Eden, in the Bible. It is a sheltered, enclosed place, with abundant nature – but only two people, a man and a woman. They have everything they need, if they will only be content.

Consider, as you read, how Ann and Loomis each regard the valley. It is Ann's home; a safe haven in the midst of the deadness. Yet, under Loomis' control, it becomes a threatening place.

Life and death

Life and death

Life, inside the valley, is seen in the abundance of nature. Ann constantly notices the details of natural sights, sounds and smells; trees and plants, animals, insects, fish and birds. The flowering crab-apple tree, the baby bird rescued in the church and the 'new fresh green' of the valley in springtime are signs of resilient life and hope. The 'deadness' outside the valley is grey and silent, with no life at all. Creatures that try to leave – like the songbirds – never return.

Robert O'Brien uses strong, visual images to show the contrast between life and death. We get a vivid picture of the rim of the valley: there is actually an 'edge' where the greenness and the deadness meet. Similarly, there is a place where the two streams merge: one is full of fish and plant life, and the other is empty, with dead creatures on its grassless banks.

There are also touching human images. Children represent new life and hope in the novel: Ann has dreamed of seeing them in the valley, but finally has to seek them outside. As for death, we have the haunting thought of the radio stations going silent one by one; the poignant picture of the Kleins' empty home, with its forgotten photograph; the patched bullet holes in the safe-suit which tell of the death of Edward.

Survival

Survival

Robert O'Brien explores two different types of survival in the book. The first simply involves providing for the **necessities of life**: food, water, shelter and so on. Ann has a few things to start her off (the house, the store), but after that she has to fend for herself. She has to grow or catch fresh food and manage without electricity. She has to ration resources which will run out (like bottled gas) and keep going those (like the animals and crops) which are renewable. She has to avoid dangers like Burden Creek. Ann is resourceful and practical and has pretty good survival skills.

Loomis cannot live off the land as Ann does: he survives by using scientific aids (like the suit and wagon) and technical knowledge. However, Ann recognises that his ideas about restoring technology and conserving resources will help them to survive in the long run. Ann's idea of survival is utilising the environment – but also sharing and co-operation.

Outside the valley, with too many people for the limited food and shelters, survival became **competitive**: people can only save themselves at the expense of others. Ann learns this from the radio, Loomis at first hand. The symbol of this struggle to survive is two people in a laboratory, with only one safe-suit between them. It is a dilemma repeated between Loomis and Ann. Within the valley, there are sufficient resources to support *both* of them: indeed, their chances of survival are even better when they work together. But Loomis cannot accept this. For him, survival is a struggle for control: kill or be killed. He makes survival in the valley competitive. Ann refuses to adopt his approach: she keeps trying to help him, even at risk to herself. She faces the kill-or-be-killed dilemma twice (first with Faro, then with Loomis himself) but each time she finds she cannot kill to save her own life.

Z for Zachariah is not directly about war, but it explores some of the causes and effects of war, through the theme of survival. It suggests that people could live in peace by sharing and working together – but fear and mistrust make them compete with each other instead. And this is what causes war in the world, just as it causes conflict in the valley.

Companionship

For a year, Ann thought she was the only person alive in the world. When Loomis arrives, she is faced with a dilemma: she longs for a companion – but what if he is crazy, or evil? Is she, in fact, better off alone?

The **need for companionship** is one factor. We know that Ann has been lonely, and she is happy helping Loomis and having someone with whom she can share the valley. Although he is a rather cold person, Loomis himself turns out to have a deep fear of being alone. There is also a practical side to companionship: people depend on each other. Ann needs Loomis' long-term thinking, just as he needs her help to survive his illness.

Fear and mistrust are the other side of the balance. Ann feels, as the man approaches, that there are 'worse things than being alone'. He is bigger and stronger than she is: what if he is crazy, mean – even a murderer? Ironically, once she has overcome her fear and befriended Loomis, she finds that he *is* all these things. It gradually becomes clear that neither Ann nor Loomis can really know or trust each other.

Companionship creates its own problems. There is the **problem of ownership and control** in a relationship. Ann naturally thinks of the valley as hers. When Loomis arrives she has to adjust to the idea of sharing everything with another person. But Loomis goes beyond sharing and begins taking possession – even of Ann herself. Finally, she calls his bluff and leaves him in sole control of 'her' valley – but miserably alone.

There is also the **problem of sex**. Both Ann and Loomis are aware that they are possibly the only man and woman left in the world. Ann finds Loomis quite attractive and thinks innocently of a proper church wedding. Loomis is neither innocent nor sensitive, and plans coldly to breed a 'colony' in the valley. He is cynical, suggestive and intimidating in his advances to Ann – and finally brutal in attempting to rape and enslave her.

In the end, Ann would rather be alone than stay with Loomis on his terms.

Art and science

Art and science

Robert O'Brien worked for many years on the *National Geographic* magazine, a famous American publication on scientific and geographical topics. His interest in such things can be seen in *Z for Zachariah*: look out for passages on weather, radioactivity, plastics and so on. However, he uses the novel to question the role of science in the modern world.

Science fiction is a type of writing that uses scientific possibilities to create conditions different from the world we know, and to imagine what life would be like in those conditions. Some science fiction authors use space or time travel to put their characters in extreme situations. O'Brien projects what would happen if there were a nuclear war; if a sheltered valley, with its own weather, could survive the destruction; and if just one radiation-proof safe-suit were in existence. He explains the science of these things just enough for us to believe they are possible: the science itself is not as important as the situation it creates. He makes it non-technical by filtering it through Ann: she is not an expert, and explains things in a simple way, according to what she knows.

Loomis is the scientist: Ann feels that his impersonal, logical mind, and his refusal to 'just accept things' are part of this training. Ann herself is interested in science, but only in a simple, practical way. While Loomis feeds his mind with information, methods and plans, Ann finds inspiration in literature, music, beauty and religious faith. The difference between them is symbolised in their attitude towards books: for Loomis, they are a source of technical knowledge, while for Ann, they are a source of courage, hope, compassion and moral values.

Scientific knowledge has its good points: as Loomis shows, it can be helpful. However, it has also created mass destruction in the war: the novel was written in 1975, when the nuclear arms race was at its height. The suit symbolises its dehumanising influence: a terrible power to survive at the expense of others. Science has also left Loomis so empty of inner resources that he can neither sustain human companionship, nor bear to be alone. Ann, with her artist's sensitivity and imagination, can do both.

Time

Time

There are two aspects of time in *Z for Zachariah*.

Time has been 'disrupted' by the **war**. For a start, there are no newspapers, radio or TV: Ann has to struggle not to lose track of time altogether. The war has caused a kind of break between the past and the present, because everything has changed: Ann has to keep reminding herself to think of things and people in the past tense. Both Ann and Loomis try to shut out the past, and to focus on the future. Look out for ideas linked to the future, like hope, fear, planning, things lasting or running out, and so on.

There is also the time-line, or 'chronology', of the book itself. A **diary** breaks time up into small chunks, usually days. The story is told by someone still in the middle of the events, not knowing how they will turn out. We share events with Ann almost as they unfold. However, note how Robert O'Brien manages to move us backwards and forwards in time to create surprise and suspense. For example, Ann's writing has to 'catch up' with events that happened since her last entry – especially if she misses a few days. So there are times when she starts an entry with a really dramatic event (like Loomis shooting her) and then goes back to explain how it happened: a mini 'flashback'. She also writes down her memories and feelings about the time before she started the diary: a realistic way of giving us background information, without requiring Ann to start writing a complete life story!

Hope

Hope

The book ends with the words 'I am hopeful'. This is a key theme for Ann, who plans optimistically, looks forward to things, and believes in luck and in the power of prayer, even when the future seems bleak. Ann hopes for many things, and we see most of them coming true (the tractor works, Mr Loomis recovers): this allows us to believe that she may actually find the place in her dream, when she sets out to find it in the deadness.

One great hope of Ann's is cruelly disappointed: her innocent dream of life with Mr Loomis. This is symbolised by the crab-apple blossom which makes her think of a summer wedding in church: later in the book, the flowers are wilted, and the tree has born a bitter fruit.

The theme of hope is balanced with fear, disappointment and desperation. There are moments when even Ann almost gives up. There is a terrible inevitability about the progress of Loomis' illness, and later about his plan to force her out of hiding – a game 'only he could win'. Yet Ann wins through both of these apparently hopeless situations. And it is Loomis who finally gives Ann her best cause to hope: he tells her he has seen birds circling in the west.

The theme of hope is also contrasted with Loomis' tendency to plan everything. Unlike Ann, he is not content to leave anything to luck, or to God: he wants to control the future himself.

Dreams

Dreams

Ann's dreams and Loomis' nightmares reveal emotions and memories which they do not let themselves think of when they are awake. Ann's deep grief for her family emerges only in dreams. It is important for her survival that she does not dwell on her loss, but this is a subtle and realistic way of letting us know that she does have deep feelings about it. Loomis' guilt and fear about Edward also emerge in his nightmares and hallucinations. There is a real sense of menace when Ann realises that this is not just a dream, but a flashback to something that really happened.

Dreams are also, for Ann, a source of guidance for the future. We do not know whether her dream of a schoolroom is just wishful thinking, or whether she is somehow 'seeing' something that is really there waiting for her. Either way, it leads her out of the valley with hope.

■ Text commentary

Chapter 1

May 20th. *Ann is afraid that someone may be coming. She has seen smoke from a camp fire, in the direction of Ogdentown – but there has been a nuclear war, and everyone in Ogdentown, and possibly everywhere else, is dead. Ann's father, brother Joseph and cousin David went to Ogdentown when the war ended, and found only bodies.* **May 21st**. *The smoke is getting nearer, and the stranger must soon notice the green of the valley: we learn that everything beyond it is barren and dead. We also learn that Ann is alone: 'all the others went away' and for a long time she thought she was the only person left alive in the world. Now that someone is coming, she is excited – but also afraid. She decides to hide.* **May 22nd**. *The stranger is just outside the valley. We learn that, after Ogdentown, Ann's family drove out again to check on the Amish farmers. The Kleins, who owned the store, went with them. Ann was supposed to stay at home with Joseph, her brother, but he was afraid of being left behind, and hid in the truck. Nobody returned. Outside the valley, everything and everyone is dead.*

'I am afraid. Someone is coming.'

Time

The first sentences plunge us right into the middle of the story. Who is the writer and why are they afraid? Curiosity make us want to read on, acting as a 'hook' to pull us into the chapter. Robert O'Brien often uses this technique: look out for other places where Ann begins a day's entry with a dramatic event, and then explains what led up to it.

In fact, the whole chapter uses mystery and surprise. Robert O'Brien does not simply explain the background to the story. He could have said that there was a nuclear war; that all life was destroyed by radiation; that only Burden

The valley

Valley, surrounded by hills, was untouched; that everyone but Ann ventured outside and died. Instead, we find all this out bit by bit. On the first page, Ann notes that 'there was no one left alive in Ogdentown'. How did you feel when you first read this? Then there is the casual phrase 'after the war ended…': Ann takes it for granted, but for us it is the first real clue to what is going on. If you read carefully, you will find lots of hints like this, gradually filling in the story like pieces in a jigsaw puzzle. Do you think the same information would have been as interesting to read without the detective work and the element of surprise?

There is another reason why the background is broken up this way. Have you ever kept a diary? You have to start somewhere. If you tried to explain everything that led up to the first entry, you would never get there! You are writing only for yourself, so you don't need to explain much – but you might refer to a past event if something reminded you of it: this is just what Ann does. Robert O'Brien's 'hook' technique is also realistic for a diary: if something really exciting happened to you on a particular day, wouldn't that be the first thing you noted down?

May 20th. We meet Ann

Ann is afraid and uncertain, but her response is to go to the church and pray, decorating the altar with flowers: she clearly draws strength from her religious faith and the beauty of nature. She is also very cool-headed, from her logical thinking about the smoke. (See how much she works out about the stranger's movements.) Ann has an amazingly matter-of-fact way of writing about the terrible things that have happened. How do you respond to this? Do you admire Ann's courage and clear thinking, or does she seem a bit 'cold'? There are hints later that she does feel grief for her family, and a deep sense of horror at the war – consider her memory of her father's hand on her head, and her inability to write about some of the things she heard on the radio. Why do you think she does not express these feelings more strongly?

May 21st. About the valley

The stranger can't help but notice the green leaves on Ann's side of Burden Hill, because on his side, everything is dead. At the end of the chapter, we learn that this is a valley, with hills on all sides and deadness all around. See what you can work out about the valley's geography. What is to the north and south? What buildings are there? Who used to live there? What kind of community was it? It might help to know that an American 'County road' is like a 'B' road in Britain (not large) and that the Amish are religious people, originally from Switzerland, who settled in America as farmers and kept a very simple life-style, with no modern technology.

The valley

The only person in the world?

Ann says her diary is 'like having someone to talk to'. What does this hint about her situation? It is made shockingly clear in her comment: 'I was pretty sure I was the only person left in the world'. Think about it. How would you feel in Ann's place? Could you get used to the idea that 'nobody… was ever going to come'?

At first, Ann hated being alone, and longed for someone to find her – but she changed her mind after hearing on the radio about the events outside. A stranger might be welcome when things are

Companionship

21

'civilised' and there are others around, but not when people are desperate and violent and you are unprotected. Ann says that 'there are worse things than being alone': what do you think she has in mind? All this explains how she feels about the approaching stranger: 'both excited and afraid'.

> Ann wonders: what if the stranger is 'someone mean, or even cruel, and brutal? A murderer?' Keep these questions in mind: see whether you think Loomis turns out to be any or all of these things, later in the book.

May 22nd. About the war

Ann mentions radioactivity and bombs, which suggests a nuclear war. (In Chapter 2, we learn that it only lasted a week.) The nearest bombs fell over 100 miles away, so the deadness may have been caused by radioactive fallout. Ann relates the simple, ominous signs: the phones going dead, and the radio stations growing silent one by one, after describing the desperate struggle amongst survivors for the remaining food supplies.

Life and death

'I am hoping'

Although Ann says she 'was' supposed to go the Teacher's College in Dean Town, she says: 'I *am* hoping to be an English teacher'. What does this say about her outlook? (If you turn to the very last paragraph of the book, you will see just how persistent it is!) The fact that she has chosen teaching as her career also shows that Ann likes to help others. We see this later in the way she looks after Loomis. (She mentions it herself later in the book.)

Ann Burden

Chapter 2

May 23rd. *Ann prepares for the stranger's arrival, removing all signs that anyone is alive in the valley. She camps in a cave, from which she can watch the house unseen. She writes a bit about how she has survived. We learn that she gets water from a nearby stream, but that there is another stream – Burden Creek – which is poisoned.* **May 24th**. *Ann watches the stranger approach. It is a man, wearing a kind of plastic-looking space suit and pulling a wagon. Ann has to decide what to do.*

Ann destroys all signs of her presence

We learn something of the life Ann has built for herself. She has kept chickens and cows, and grown vegetables. She has had 'good luck', but also 'taken good care of them': she has been taught to live off the land by respecting and looking after it. As well as setting free the animals and destroying the garden, she removes the flowers from the church: a reminder

The valley

that her life is more than physical survival. As she surveys her valley from the cave, it seems a very simple setting: just a house, a store, a church, a brook and a road. What does this say about Ann's life?

Ann the survivor

Ann carefully writes dates and times in her diary, but here she admits she is

Time

not really sure of them. Keeping time may not have occurred to you as a problem, but it shows how the most basic things were disrupted by the war. (How do *you* know what day it is?) Ann needs to hold on to familiar landmarks, like her birthday. Her system for marking and checking the date is precise and ingenious: how has her upbringing helped her?

Ann says she 'could write a lot' of other things about survival, but only gives a few examples, like staying warm and getting water. She shows great foresight and good sense: notice how she cuts firewood well before winter. She is equally sensible preparing for the stranger's arrival – and cautious enough to go armed.

> **Guns** are a symbol of mistrust and conflict in the book. Note that although Ann is a good shot, she does not like them. We will find out about Loomis' attitude in the next chapter…

The two streams

One stream flows from a spring in the hills: it is clear and full of fish, and feeds

Life and death

the pond. The other, Burden Creek, is bigger and closer to the house – but the water is poisoned, and kills everything near it: it flows from outside. This is important in the plot when Loomis, unaware that there are two streams, bathes in the poisoned one. It is also symbolic: water from inside the valley is pure and life-sustaining, but water from outside brings in poison and death – the effects of war. What does this suggest about the 'insider', Ann, and the 'outsider' who is about to enter the valley?

Ann is a girl!

Ann Burden

At last Ann describes herself, and we know for sure that she is a girl. Have you felt, up to now, that you were reading a girl's diary or a boy's? Why did you think so?

The stranger arrives

The stranger is alien, unnatural, faceless and barely human in his mask and all-covering suit. What effect do you think his appearance has on Ann? Notice

that she was right to sense all along that it was a 'he', not a 'she' or 'they': it is indeed 'a man, one man alone'. Following our discovery that Ann is a girl, what would be the good and bad points about the stranger's being a man?

Chapter 3

May 24th (continued). *The man finds the green valley. He tests carefully for radiation, then removes his mask and cheers for joy. Still cautious, he descends to the house and searches for signs of life. He pitches a tent made of the plastic-like material: Ann realises it must be radiation-proof.* **May 25th.** *The stranger hears the animals, and explores. He finds the pond, with its living fish, and visits the store. Hot and tired, he jumps into the stream near the house, unaware that it is poisoned. Ann, watching secretly, worries that his mistake might kill him.*

The stranger enters the valley

The stranger's feelings are clear. Look for signs in his actions of surprise and excitement, then hesitation, self-control and caution, and finally joy and relief when he realises the valley is safe.

The man of science

Art and science

The stranger tests everything with gadgets which Ann identifies as Geiger counters, devices for measuring radiation. He uses science to protect himself, while Ann has had to use only common sense. However, Ann has successfully avoided the radioactive creek: it is the stranger, for all his technology, who falls foul of it.

The stranger becomes human

John Loomis

Companionship

The stranger seems more human from the moment he cheers. Note that he has a 'nice' voice and a slightly fragile appearance, which Ann thinks is 'rather poetic': do you find this reassuring? (Remember that Ann has feared someone bigger and stronger than herself.) Ann suddenly feels a rush of emotion: what do you think this might be?

Ann controls herself: she is still cautious. See how she refers to 'my house', 'my wood' and 'my chickens': the stranger is an outsider in her valley. But she also starts to feel that it is 'companionable' to have someone around.

May 25th. 'It may be that he has made a mistake.'

Robert O'Brien again uses a 'hook' to arouse our curiosity. Ann notes the important thing first: the stranger has made a mistake. What is it? We are left in suspense while she goes back to explain events in the proper order.

The stranger explores

The man is not at home on the land like Ann. Note the casual way she writes

Survival

about the animals' habits and crop rotation. Contrast the stranger's behaviour: what does he do that is not accepted practice on a farm?

Loomis, like Ann, keeps a gun handy. We learn here that Ann has not fired a gun once, since before the war – but the first thing Loomis does in the valley is shoot a chicken and try to shoot a rabbit. What does this suggest about the way Ann and Loomis regard living things? Do you think either of them would shoot another person if they had to? We will see, later in the book.

The stranger's mistake

Perhaps Ann should have warned the stranger about Burden Creek. He was hot and tired, and did not know about the two streams. But he was also careless and unobservant: Ann describes the creek as quite obviously dead.

Life and death

As well as the details of the creek, note that 'the songbirds are all gone': why might they remind you of Ann's family? The chapter ends with a further horrific hint about the war: the enemy used nerve gas, bacteria and other 'anti-personnel weapons' – a cynical way of saying 'weapons intended to kill people'.

Chapter 4

May 25th (continued). *David's dog Faro turns up after a year in the hills. He accepts food from the stranger, then follows Ann's tracks to the cave: Ann worries that he might give her away. She is still torn between loneliness and fear.* **May 26th.** *The stranger sets out to explore the rest of the valley. At the southern end, he finds the place where the clear stream meets Burden Creek: he realises that there are two streams, and that one is poisoned. Having seen that the valley is surrounded by deadness, he turns back. He begins to be very sick, and crawls back to his tent.*

Faro returns

Companionship

Faro was mentioned in Chapter 2 as having run away in search of David and, presumably, died – but now he is back. The way Ann describes him gives him lots of realistic dog personality: loyal, affectionate, suspicious, excited. You might also notice how Faro reflects Ann's dilemma about the stranger: he has survived on his own, but prefers companionship; he mistrusts the stranger, but is drawn to him by necessity. (How long do you think Ann will be able to stay in the hills without access to the farm or store?) Note, too, that Faro is a hunting dog, and that Ann fears he will 'betray' her by leading the man to the cave: her fears will be realised when she is *back* in the cave, later in the book...

The stranger seems 'quite nice'

John Loomis

The stranger is further 'humanised' in this chapter. Think about his friendliness to Faro, and the way he looks when he cuts his hair and beard, and when he dresses in normal clothes. Do you feel that Ann is *looking* for reasons to think he is a 'nice' person?

Hopes and fears

We learn that Ann has hoped and prayed not just for a companion, but a

Hope

partner: a man with whom she can have a family in the valley. As she says herself, this is a 'simple' hope. On the other hand, she recalls what she heard on the radio: the fight for survival has made people desperate and selfish. Robert O'Brien builds up the threatening words here: see if you can spot them. Note carefully what Ann's fears are: is Loomis going to be, or do, these things? Or will he fulfil her hopes?

May 26th. It is Sunday

Ann Burden

We see something of Ann's religious nature. How does she keep Sunday as a special day, and why? The books of Psalms and Ecclesiastes, which she particularly likes in the Bible, are very poetic and speak deeply about human nature and values, which suggests something about what Ann gets out of them.

The stranger explores further

The valley

Some final pieces of valley geography fall into place. We learn that the 'gap' at the south end is covered by overlapping hills: the valley is enclosed on all sides, and outside wind and weather do not affect it. What does this help to explain? (See Chapter 6 for a technical explanation.)

Life and death

We also see, in a very vivid picture of life and death, the place where the two streams merge before flowing out of the gap. The poisoned/outside creek contaminates the pure/inside stream. In what ways do you think Ann could be 'contaminated' by the stranger from the outside world? What 'poison' might he have brought in with him?

As the stranger surveys the deadness, Ann enjoys the beauty of the valley. Note the vivid images of life, just shadowed by the death of the songbirds. This increases the tension when the stranger, immediately afterwards, falls ill.

Chapter 5

*May 27th. Ann fears the man may be dying. She dreams about her family, and realises how much she wants him to live. She decides to check on him. **May 28th.** Ann finds the stranger feverish and muttering about someone called Edward. She nurses him through the night. In the morning, she tells him about Burden Creek. He gets her to check it with a Geiger counter and realises that he has radiation poisoning. He tells Ann that he will be very ill, and that he may die. Ann decides to look after him in the house.*

May 27th. Ann dreams about her family

Ann dreams that it is her father in the tent, and then that her whole family

Dreams

has returned. She feels a great shock of joy. This dream hints at a grief and longing which Ann holds back when she is awake. (Later, when she finds herself thinking similar thoughts, she says that she has 'banned' herself from wishing or imagining that her family are back: it would be too painful and pointless, and would only weaken her for her struggle to survive.)

Ann comes out of hiding

Companionship

The dream also makes Ann realise that she has not got used to loneliness after all: she cannot bear the thought of being alone again. The stranger's illness tips the balance between caution and companionship. Instead of being afraid *of* the stranger, she is afraid *for* him.

May 28th. Ann meets the stranger – and Edward

Ann's description of the sick man's symptoms are detailed and realistic, and show just how brave and sensible she has to be to help him. Could *you* have coped?

The man's first words are mysterious: 'Edward'. Then 'Bullets. It won't stop…' Try to finish the sentence: do you have enough information to do so? (Loomis finishes it for us in Chapter 11…)

Ann nurses the stranger

Art and science

Ann admits she knows little about medicine. However helpless this makes her feel, she is brave, determined and practical about nursing the sick man. He approaches his own illness in a more scientific way: he gets Ann to check the creek for radiation, and tells her about radiation poisoning in quite technical terms. (Since Ann is not a scientist, he explains most of them to her – which is O'Brien's way of explaining them to us as well.)

The man will develop a high fever and anaemia (a deficiency in the red blood cells) and his body will lose its resistance to other illnesses: depending how much radiation he has absorbed, he may die. What do you think enables the man to be calm and 'matter-of-fact' about his illness? (See, later in the book, whether you think he is equally calm when faced with things that he knows less about.) What helps Ann to be calm? Notice that he is technical and almost impersonal in talking about his illness, while Ann is practical and caring.

John Loomis

> We have reached the end of a distinct phase in the story. So far, Ann has been alone and hiding in her cave, fearful that the stranger might be a murderer, or might enslave her. As Chapter 6 opens, she is back in her house, and no longer alone: the second phase explores her relationship with Loomis. The final phase starts in Chapter 19, with Ann alone and hiding in her cave, knowing that Loomis is a murderer and is trying to enslave her. What do you notice about the structure of the book?

Self-test (Questions) Chapters 1–5

Uncover the plot
Delete two of the three alternatives given, to find the correct plot. Beware possible misconceptions and muddles.

Ann lives in Ogden/Burden/Claypole Valley. There has been a fire/war/plague. Ann's family and the Burdens/Kleins/Faros have died/fled/escaped, but the valley is grey/green/brown. Then Ann sees cars/birds/smoke, and feels 'both excited and eager/afraid/alone'. A stranger arrives in a 'plastic-/metal-/glassy-looking' suit, and Ann decides to approach/watch/shoot him. From her tent/tree/cave, she sees him explore the deadness/farm/valley. He even shoots a rabbit/dog/chicken. He finds minnows/dead fish/radioactivity in the pond, and jumps into the pond/pond stream/Burden Creek. Next day, he walks north/south/west towards Burden Hill/Claypole Ridge/the gap, where the roads/streams/hills join. Returning, he becomes worried/ill/excited. Ann wants him to live/leave/die, and goes to the house/church/tent to help. The man says: 'Ann/Edward/Loomis'. He has food/chemical/radiation poisoning.

Who? What? Why? When? Where? How?
1 Whose name (out of the living characters) do we learn in these chapters?
2 Who are David, Joseph, Faro and the Kleins?
3 What does Ann do to hide the fact that she has been living in the valley?
4 What did Ann want to do after she left school?
5 Where in the valley is Burden Hill, and where is the gap?
6 Why does Ann write her diary, and why has she started to write it properly?
7 Why did the others in the valley 'go away'?

8 Why does the stranger bathe in the poisoned stream?
9 How does Ann know which stream is pure and which is poisoned?
10 How has Burden Valley survived untouched?

Who's who?

From your knowledge of the characters in the book, identify the following people.

1 Who 'prayed all this morning' in church, and who 'stayed a few minutes'?
2 Who has a gun, and who fires one?
3 Who 'seems to be adopting the man'?
4 Who misses the songbirds?

Natural science

Science, as opposed to nature, has already become an important theme. Let's explore…

1 How has Ann used nature to survive?
2 What technology has been lost in the valley, and what problems does this pose?
3 How has the stranger used science to survive and protect himself?
4 What other uses of science in the outside world – bad or good – do we hear about?

I want to be alone

Will the stranger be a friend or a threat to Ann? Let's explore…

1 How did Ann first feel about being left alone, and what changed her mind?
2 What words does Ann use in Chapter 1 to describe the worst sort of person that might come?
3 In Chapter 4, why has Ann hoped for someone to come? What has she dreamed about them?
4 What makes Ann overcome her fear of the stranger?
5 Find three things that make the man seem 'attractive and friendly' (as Ann later calls him).

War game

Ann does not simply describe the war, but gives us scattered details. Let's explore…

1 Find four 'signs' of the war that have reached the valley in Chapter 1.
2 Find three things that suggest what kind of a war it was.
3 Find three things that suggest that the world outside is still radioactive.
4 Find three examples of how war has made people behave. What fourth example is hinted at?

Chapter 6

May 29th. *The man seems better. Ann moves him into the house, and they talk. His name is John Loomis. He was a chemist, working on a secret government project to develop a radiation-proof plastic. He says he was alone in a sheltered laboratory with food supplies and the test model of the safe-suit when the war broke out. After three months, he took the suit out to search for survivors and eventually found the valley. Ann asks him about Edward, the name he called out in the tent: Loomis says he was a colleague in the laboratory.*

Ann has company

Ann says she just likes having someone to talk to — but notice how self-conscious she is about her appearance. Can you find other clues that she might be aware of Loomis as a man? How does Loomis behave towards her? When Ann says 'You can lean on me', she sums up their relationship at this stage. It seems natural to her, but how do you think Loomis feels, being so dependent on another person: a stranger — and a girl?

Companionship

Ann tells Loomis about the valley

Ann's story gives a further shocking hint of what she has been through: for months after the war, she expected the deadness to 'creep in from outside'.

Ann says the valley has its own weather: Loomis says a 'meteorological enclave' (the same thing, in technical language) is a 'theoretical possibility'. Ann, not being scientific, thinks it silly to call it a possibility, when they are actually in it! She notes that scientists never 'just accept things' but 'try to figure them out': is this how Loomis thinks?

The valley

> It is actually unlikely that such a valley *would* survive, given the real effects of nuclear war — and if it did, people could not stand right on the 'edge' of the deadness. (Scientists now know, for example, about the 'nuclear winter': cold and dark, caused by dust and smoke from the explosions blocking out the sunlight. The valley would not escape this effect.) But Ann's non-technical viewpoint does not let us worry too much about scientific accuracy. Robert O'Brien asks us to play along, to pretend for a while that a single valley could survive untouched, so that he can tell a dramatic story. This is called the **willing suspension of disbelief**: we choose to believe the science is true, for the purposes of the story.

Loomis tells his story

Loomis' story is all recent career history — nothing very personal. He is clearly

absorbed in science and we assume that he was a top man in his field, since he was invited to work with a Nobel prize winner. Unlike the scientific Loomis, Ann does not find the new plastic 'too exciting a discovery' in itself — but she has a clear-sighted grasp of its value to the government. She sees that in the suit, science was being used to lengthen the war.

Art and science

Do you think the scientists — Loomis and Kylmer — looked at it this way?

'On the night the bombing began...'

We learn later that this is not the whole truth about what happened that night. Loomis was *not* alone in the laboratory, as he claims.

Survival

Loomis had to use all his scientific knowledge to survive. He also saw the brutal, selfish side of survival that Ann heard about on the radio: at the Air Force command post, people had killed each other for spaces in the fallout shelter. (The story of what really happened in the laboratory will reveal that Loomis himself was involved in a similar fight for life.) Loomis has seen the horror of war: 'grey wasteland, empty highways and dead cities and towns'. Do you get any sense of how he feels about this? Do you feel sorry for him at all?

> Loomis notes that **fallout shelters** were built on the theory that radioactivity wears off after a certain time – and it has not done so. What is the implication of this for any survivors? It certainly suggests that science has let them down rather badly…

Who was Edward?

John Loomis

Notice Loomis' shocked reaction when Ann asks about Edward. Is it explained, as he claims, by surprise that she knows the name, or do you feel that there is more to it than that? Robert O'Brien is very gradually building up a sense of mystery around the character of Edward. This technique of witholding information is realistic (since these are things Ann has no way of knowing) and also creates suspense.

Chapter 7

June 3rd. *Four days have passed. On the first, Loomis is no worse, and Ann starts planning for two. She replants the garden and Loomis suggests how they can get the tractor working. They watch a sunset together and Ann plays the piano. That night, Loomis has a nightmare about Edward.*

Time

The diary entry is dated June 3rd, but this is only the day when Ann finds time to write it. Chapters 7–9 actually cover the events of May 31st–June 2nd: Ann catches up with the events of June 3rd itself in Chapter 10. This creates the effect of a 'flashback': Ann is sitting with the sick Loomis on June 3rd, looking *back* over the past four days.

Planning for two

Companionship

After a year alone, Ann has to adjust to having someone else around. What aspects of her life does she change to fit in with Loomis? (Think about her cooking, her appearance and her after-dinner habits.) What would you do – or not bother to do – if you were left completely to yourself?

Ann doubles the garden because there will be two people to feed from now on. She is happy to share everything with Loomis: she is not selfish or possessive about what the valley provides. (Unfortunately, as we later discover, Loomis does not have the same attitude.) This also shows Ann's tendency to be hopeful and positive, as she works on the assumption that Loomis will recover from his illness.

Ann Burden

Loomis contributes

It seems obvious to Loomis that the petrol pumps can be worked by hand.

Ann feels stupid not to have thought of it: in fact, she is just not technically-minded like Loomis. (Look out for signs that Loomis looks down on Ann's non-scientific thinking, and ways in which he deliberately makes her feel stupid about it, later in the book.) Even so, his suggestion – which is all the help he can give, at the moment – is sensible, and a fresh source of hopes and plans for Ann.

Art and science

A moment of companionship

Loomis and Ann watch a sunset together and he rests his hand on her shoulder. She feels proud to be of help to him. Is there anything about this moment that makes you feel uneasy? Remember how Ann feared that someone bigger and stronger would come. Later in the book, when Loomis is recovering, hints of his growing strength are distinctly threatening.

Companionship

Who gets bored?

Loomis feels bored, and Ann is surprised: there is so much to do, she has

'forgotten about being bored'. What does Ann do for entertainment? There are suggestions in her after-dinner entertainment for Loomis. He, unlike Ann, seems to lack the ability or desire to fill his own time creatively. (What would *you* do if there were no electricity: no TV, radio, video or computers?)

Ann Burden

After Ann plays the piano for him, Loomis says 'This is the best evening I have ever spent'. What might he have particularly enjoyed about it? It suggests that Loomis' home life must have been rather deprived.

A for Adam

The hymns remind Ann of Sunday School, and she feels a kind of 'homesickness' for the days before the war. Note what she says about Adam and Zachariah in *The Bible Letter Book*. Why is *Z for Zachariah* the title of the novel?

> Ann and Loomis are like **Adam and Eve** (see pages 6–7 of this guide): the only man and woman in the world. But Loomis is not Adam: he is Zachariah. What difference does this make? Think about the first man, innocently starting out in a newly-created world: how would he face the future? Now think about the last man, living with the memories – and guilt – of a world newly destroyed.

Loomis dreams about Edward

Dreams

There are some fairly clear clues as to what Loomis is dreaming about, from his side of the conversation. See if you can fill in Edward's side of it. What do you think happened? Loomis' shout and 'terrible groan' suggest that the event is painful and traumatic for him.

Chapter 8

June 3rd (continued). *On the second morning, Ann happily gathers fresh greens for a salad and is struck by the beauty of a crab-apple tree in blossom. She thinks about marrying Loomis in church and having children. Meanwhile, Loomis is making plans to generate electricity. He wants to go fishing with Ann, but collapses: it is the anaemia. He retires to bed, where he pores over books on mechanics.*

An inspiring dream

Dreams

This is the first of Ann's dreams which seem 'helpful, as if they came with a purpose'. It is a memory of her mother, but it also inspires her to find greens for a fresh salad. Later, this kind of dream will lead Ann out of the valley.

'It was cool, but still and pleasant...'

Life and death

Despite everything, Ann still has the ability to feel pleasure, even joy: her life is not just survival. The scene in the fields is full of excitement, life and growth. The way Ann describes it shows that although she is knowledgeable and practical about nature and the land, she still appreciates its beauty and mystery.

A summer wedding?

Hope

The apple blossom makes Ann think of a church wedding in summer, and she reveals her thoughts of marrying Loomis and having children. Given that he is a stranger, and has radiation sickness, this is a good example of Ann's hopeful nature. In fact, a family with Loomis becomes the central hope in her life.

Ann is old-fashioned and innocent about relationships, as her one, rather prim 'date' shows. (Have you noticed what she *calls* the man she plans to marry, even to herself?) However, she is not just being conventional in wanting a proper church ceremony: marriage is a solemn and religious idea for Ann.

> The **crab-apple blossom** symbolises Ann's hopes of a future with Loomis. She takes blossoms to his sick room, but he never seems to notice them – and when he is very ill (and has been revealed as a murderer), the blossoms have wilted and fallen: Ann's hopes are spoiled. You might also note that the crab-apple has a sour fruit: what does this say about the likely 'fruition' or outcome of the relationship between Ann and Loomis?

Fishing – or farm mechanics?

After Ann's enjoyment of nature, we find Loomis planning to dam Burden

Creek to power an electricity generator. Ann welcomes the suggestion because it will make life pleasanter – but Loomis' scientific ideas and plans already seem rather alien to Ann's way of using the valley's natural resources to survive.

Art and science

Loomis shows a rather touching eagerness to go fishing with Ann. What do we sense about his boyhood life? He never gets to go, and instead starts poring over the technical information in *The Farm Mechanic*: do you feel this is more natural to him?

Chapter 9

June 3rd (continued). *On the third morning, Loomis shows Ann how to get petrol from the pumps at the store, and she gets the tractor going. She starts to plan for full self-sufficiency, and happily sets about ploughing a suitable field. But that night, Loomis' temperature soars.*

The tractor works

Ann Burden

Ann thanks *The Farm Mechanic* for her success with the petrol pumps – but would Loomis have known what to do with the tractor? His technical book-knowledge contrasts with Ann's farming knowledge and practical competence: look how confidently she plans the ploughing and planting.

Surviving – or living?

Survival

Loomis' matter-of-factness about the tractor also contrasts with Ann's excitement. To him, it is only a means to an end, while to Ann it is a 'triumph', a source of fresh purpose and hope. See how Robert O'Brien links Ann's work in the fields with the life and nature around her, with her love of music and poetry, and specifically with her hopes of the future with Loomis.

Loomis is, in a way, quite right to be cool and calculating about survival. Ann realises now that the endless supplies in the store are an illusion: they will soon run out or spoil. She has tried to ignore the fact – but Loomis has already considered it. Where Ann hopes, Loomis plans. Look out for examples of how he carefully saves things for later use, like the V belt on the petrol pump. Which approach is likely to be most helpful for survival – and for the survivors' quality of life?

Chapter 10

June 3rd (continued). *Ann finally has time to write up the last three days' events, because Loomis is very ill and she dare not leave the house. He is weak and distressed, and seems to fret when she is not there. Returning from a brief trip to the store, she finds a delirious Loomis outside, shooting at the upstairs windows: he imagined Edward was in the house. Back in bed, he reminds himself that Edward is dead. Ann is worried.*

'It's started'

John Loomis

Suddenly, Loomis is 'tired and frail' and 'really afraid': the critical part of his illness has begun. What details does Robert O'Brien use to make us feel sorry for Loomis here? (Look at the quiet, kindly way he speaks to Ann.)

Ann Burden

Ann comes under increasing pressure in this chapter, as Loomis' illness makes growing demands on her time and courage. She says that 'When he got weaker, I got stronger'. Do you react this way when someone needs your help? Even so, Ann is anxious about Loomis and is very sensitive to his fear and suffering.

'Poor Ann Burden. You're going to wish I had never come.'

Ann normally 'hopes', but here – perhaps because she feels helpless – she

Hope

'wishes'. She wishes she knew more about nursing. She wishes for a future with Loomis: note that her earlier hopes seem foolish and sad. She also wishes she had tried to warn him about the creek. (Does he blame her? See how reassuring he is, in the midst of his own crisis.)

Ironically, Loomis' prediction also comes true: Ann *will* wish, later, that he had never come to the valley – but not because he is a troublesome patient, which is what he means here.

'It's the fever. It makes me imagine things.'

Loomis does not like to be left alone. Is he just weak and fearful, or does he

John Loomis

seem more worried about what Ann is doing when she is away? The second time she leaves him, to go to the store, his fear and confusion are extreme. We learn that he is trying to shoot at Edward: we also learn that Edward is dead. Ann does not connect the two things – but why might they be ominous?

The incident where **Loomis shoots at 'Edward'** in his delirium is the first violent crisis Ann faces with him: for a moment he actually points the gun at her, but she stays calm and he comes to his senses. This is mirrored in the last chapter of the book, when Loomis deliberately threatens to kill Ann – who really is in role of Edward this time, having stolen the suit. Can you think of other moments of violence in the book?

Chapter 11

June 4th. *Loomis' fever reaches its peak. He seems to fear that Edward will steal the suit: Ann brings it in from the wagon. In Loomis' nightmare, he and Edward are trapped in the lab; Edward has a family outside and wants to borrow the suit to search for them, Loomis refuses; Edward steals the suit and tries to leave; Loomis shoots him. Ann finds bullet holes in the suit, and realises that this was no nightmare, but something that really happened. Loomis is now on the brink of death, and all Ann can do is pray for him in the church. Even if he is a murderer, she wants him to live.*

'...something vague and dreadful'

Dreams

Robert O'Brien increases the tension as the story of Loomis and Edward gradually unfolds. At first it is Edward who seems to be threatening a terrified Loomis: he cries 'Stay back, Edward. Stay back'.

'The suit. He'll steal the suit.'

This is the next clue. How do you feel about Edward by this time? Even Ann half expects to see him 'prowling around'.

'...not just for twenty-four hours, Edward.'

Finally, we hear the whole story. Can you now fill in what Edward is saying,

Survival

from Loomis' replies? In any case, Ann explains why he wanted to take the suit. Loomis' argument is basically that it would be (a) risky and (b) pointless, and the suit is too important to risk for any one individual. Ann understands the logic of Loomis' decision – but she still identifies with 'poor Edward' and his 'wild hope' of saving people he loved. Where do your sympathies lie?

'One suit, and two people. That was the situation.' This is a symbolic, simplified version of **the survival dilemma**, which we have already seen at the radio station and the Air Force base. Edward and Loomis were trapped in a situation where each could live only by killing the other. Remember Loomis' observation about fallout shelters, in Chapter 6: the food, water or air would run out before the radiation went away, so whoever was left in the shelter would die. Can you see any parallels with the situation of Ann and Loomis trapped together in the valley? What are the differences?

'...it won't stop bullets.'

Ann remembers Loomis' first words to her (see Chapter 5). How does the

John Loomis

completion of a simple sentence change things? We now know that Loomis is capable of killing if his plans – or his own survival – are threatened.

In Chapter 1, Ann's worst fear was that the valley might be found by a 'murderer': look what she calls Loomis at the end of Chapter 11.

There is nothing more Ann can do

Hope

Ann still does not give up hoping and caring for Loomis. When there is nothing else she can do, she goes to the church to pray for him – and to find peace and courage for herself. Do you think Loomis is a praying kind of person? (We shall soon find out.)

Chapter 12

June 5th. *Loomis is barely hanging on. Exhausted and anxious, Ann returns to the church, where she rescues a baby crow which has fallen from its nest. Back home, she reads to the unconscious Loomis, and frets about what happened with Edward. Was Loomis right or wrong? Either way, it is a terrible secret for Ann to carry alone.* **June 6th.** *Ann has almost given up hope. She goes to the church, then waits by Loomis' quiet bedside.*

'I said a prayer, and crept closer.'

Ann Burden

This is the worst point in Loomis' illness. How does Ann respond to it? She gives Loomis practical, tender care, but also something of herself. She tries to reach him through the things that are most important to her, and that give her strength, hope and comfort. Poetry is one example: see what others you can find.

The baby crow

This incident somehow gives Ann hope. She has been worrying about the

Edward/Loomis business: perhaps the bird clarifies the issues for her. Whatever Loomis has done, he – like the helpless bird – needs her care and compassion at this moment: life is important. See how tenderly she describes and handles the bird. The baby crow is also a symbol of new life in the valley,

Life and death set against Loomis' nearness to death.

> **Birds** are an omen of good luck to Ann. She associates them with prayers, so they also suggest her faith and hope. Bear this in mind, when you read Loomis' last words to Ann at the very end of the book: birds are the only sign that Ann's hopes of finding life are not completely unfounded.

'I suppose I have to accept the idea...'

Ann thinks through the issues of Loomis' killing of Edward. It is personally important to her to understand what happened, because of what she has hoped about Loomis and herself. Remember, Loomis is the only friend Ann now has: how would you feel in her place?

There are several arguments in Loomis' favour. Shooting Edward was, in

effect, self-defence: without the suit, Loomis would have died in the lab. Also, he may have been thinking unselfishly about the suit's importance for the human race: it was the only way survivors could make contact with each other. Edward may have been too thoughtless or selfish to think of these things –

John Loomis but he may not: he may have been 'honest and sensible'. Ann does not take the easy way out: she considers the possibility that Loomis was just selfish and desperate, and killed Edward to keep the suit for himself. She admits that she simply does not know Loomis well enough to decide.

> Either way, the **murder of Edward** is a terrible secret for Ann to share, without Loomis knowing. What would you do in her place: would you ask him about it, straight out – or pretend that you knew nothing? Ann takes the latter course: she does not challenge Loomis about Edward until the very last confrontation.

Chapter 13

June 7th. *Loomis is better, though still unconscious. Thinking about books, Ann wonders if she might use the safe-suit to get some from Ogdentown – but this reminds her of Edward's fate.* **June 8th.** *Loomis is completely helpless, but showing signs of life. Ann fulfils her long-held plan to get the wood stove from the barn to the kitchen: she has a sense of hope and purpose again.*

Anne's purpose in life

Ann considered a nursing career because it involved 'helping people who need help'. What does this say about her? She chose teaching because it combined 'helping' with opportunities for reading, which she loves.

Hope

It has been hard for Ann to give up her plans and ambitions. Notice how she puts it: 'I am not going to *be* anything... or go anywhere or do anything except what I do here.' Has Ann lost her sense of purpose in life? How does she maintain it? Consider the assembly of the stove (June 8th): it is something she has planned for a long time, and now achieved. Note how proud she feels about it.

We learn later that Ann has not, in fact, quite let go of her hope of being a teacher. It re-emerges in her dream of the classroom which leads her out of the valley, at the end of the book.

Books – and temptation

We already know that Ann likes poetry and the Bible, and turns to them in

Art and science

moments of both joy and stress. Here we find out just how important books and reading are to her. The thought of them gets Ann really excited about the possibilities of the safe-suit for the first time: note that its inventor, Loomis, is 'not much of a reader'. Ann is discerning: she likes 'any good writing', and we can tell, from the authors she mentions in the book, that she loves the classics of English literature. Mental refinement balances her practical farming skills.

> We know that, for Loomis, the **suit** represents a scientific breakthrough and an important part of his plans for long-term human survival. Ann, on the other hand, thinks simply but creatively about how the suit could be used to enhance the quality of life. Like Edward, with his 'wild hope' of saving the people he loved, Ann has personal needs and hopes of the suit, which would seem pointless and trivial to Loomis – as we see in Chapter 15.

When Ann thinks about borrowing the suit and going to get the books herself, she remembers Edward. Why does this give her a 'jolt'?

> In Chapter 10, Ann said that as Loomis got weaker, she got stronger. This sums up the central phase of the novel so far. But from this point on, the process is reversed: Loomis is gaining strength again. The balance changes. You will find incidents from Chapters 6–13 repeated in Chapters 14–18: like mirror images, they reflect the changes brought about by Loomis' recovery.

Self-test (Questions) Chapters 6–13

Uncover the plot

Delete two of the three alternatives given, to find the correct plot. Beware possible misconceptions and muddles.

The stranger's name is John/James/Joseph Loomis. He was a physicist/chemist/biologist at Ithaca/New York/Cornell University, working on a radiation-proof metal/plastic/rubber called polymer/polapoly/polarity with Professor Cornell/Klymer/Kylmer when the war began. Ann works in the garden/tractor/truck and Loomis suggests getting books/petrol/water. Ann notices a cherry/orange/crab-apple tree in bloom, and thinks of leaving/marrying/feeding Loomis. She gets the truck/tractor/generator going and ploughs/plants/sings happily – but Loomis is suddenly gone/better/worse. He dreams about food/Edward/Ann. Ann discovers that in the Air Force base/fallout shelter/laboratory, Loomis shot Kylmer/civilians/Edward to keep the food/suit/secret for himself. Ann prays that Loomis will die/live/confess.

Who? What? Why? When? Where? How?

1 Who are Mary and Billy?
2 Who is Professor Kylmer?
3 What two things suggest that Loomis has not had much 'fun' in his life?
4 What dreams are featured in these chapters?
5 Where does 'Z for Zachariah' come from, and why is it relevant?
6 Where does Ann want to get married, and how?
7 Why did the government want polapoly developed?
8 Why has Ann wanted to be a teacher?
9 How had the people at the Air Force base died?
10 How do Ann and Loomis each react to getting the tractor going?

Who said that?

From your knowledge of the characters in the book, identify the following speakers.

1 Who says: 'I had forgotten about being bored'?
2 Who says: 'V belts are useful, and we have nowhere to buy any more'?
3 Who says: 'It seemed like a good profession, since your whole occupation is helping people'?
4 Who says: 'I suppose that's a theoretical possibility. But the odds–'?
5 Who says: 'I did not know what else to do, so I thought I might pray'?

All about Edward

1 Why did Edward want to take the suit?
2 Why did Loomis think it would be pointless?
3 Why did Loomis think it would be wrong, even if Edward meant to bring it back?
4 Why might both of them have wanted the suit for more selfish reasons?
5 When pleading failed, what did Edward try to do?

Clashing symbols

What ideas are represented by the following?

1 The crab-apple blossom
2 The safe-suit
3 The baby crow
4 The wood-fuelled stove
5 Books

In two minds

1   Find three things Loomis does that show him as a 'scientist' or technically-minded person.
2   Find three things Ann does that show her as an 'artistic' and spiritual person.
3   What do you notice about how they use their different 'gifts' at this stage of the book?

Chapter 14

June 15th. *It is Ann's sixteenth birthday, and she and Loomis celebrate together. For a week, he has been slowly improving, although he is still weak. Ann has begun work in the fields again, and Loomis has begun to take a rather impatient interest in her progress.*

Ann's diary entries get further apart: she has to catch up on several days' events at a time. This helps to build up tension, suggesting that Ann's life is getting hectic and out of control. It also creates surprise and suspense, as Ann first hints at dramatic events and then goes back to explain what led up to them. In a way, it is like glimpsing the future – as well as watching a flashback!

Time

One of the best of weeks

Loomis' recovery at first seems a hopeful thing, to be celebrated along with

Ann's birthday. Look for the small details that express Ann's happiness and excitement, and her feelings about Loomis. Remember how she tried to cook a romantic dinner with candles just before he became really ill (Chapter 8)? This is a kind of mirror image of that meal, with Loomis just recovered.

Hope

Ann describes Loomis' improvement like that of a baby going through the stages ('milestones') of seeing, sitting up, talking, walking and eating solid food for the first time. This emphasises Ann's caring nature, and Loomis' dependence on her. However, it also suggests that he will not be dependent for ever: babies grow up. What things does Loomis insist on doing for himself in this chapter?

Loomis scolds Ann about the delay in the planting

This incident makes Ann realise that an important change has taken place. She

has regarded the tractor and the farming – the whole valley – as her responsibility. But now, for the first time, Loomis knows he is going to live: he has begun to regard the valley 'as much his' as Ann's. How does she react to this – and what does it say about her as a person?

Companionship

Loomis' annoyance also reflects his approach to survival –

John Loomis

and his attitude to life. What two reasons does Ann give for having fallen behind with the planting? What does it say about Loomis that he regards these things – which are so important to Ann – as a waste of time?

'No,' he said, quite fiercely. 'I can do it.'

The chapter ends where it began: with Ann's birthday. Now that you have read about it, do you feel it really has been 'one of the best of weeks' for Ann? Notice the contrast between Loomis' planning activity after dinner (technical diagrams, we assume) and Ann's (a cake for the celebration).

Chapter 15

June 22nd. *Another week has passed, during which Loomis has taught himself to walk again. He wishes he had more technical books, and Ann mentions her plan to go to Ogdentown library: Loomis forbids it. He says they must start planning seriously for long-term survival in the valley.*

Loomis learns to walk

John Loomis

Walking is a symbol of Loomis' growing strength and independence of Ann's help. Here, she feels proud of him – but she will soon feel increasingly threatened. (See the very end of Chapter 16.) Look out, in the following chapters, for signs of Loomis' progress, and their effect on Ann.

'I wish I had a book'

Art and science

Ann and Loomis are contrasted through their attitude to reading. What books does Loomis want, and what does he hope to get out of them? What about Ann? Loomis feels that getting novels is a foolish use of the suit: it should be used only for technical books, and other serious survival priorities. Do you feel that Loomis needs to 'loosen up' a bit?

Books have become a symbol of what the characters want from life. It is not just that Loomis finds literature uninteresting to him personally: he cannot see any point or value to it at all. There is no room in his survival plans for imagination, beauty or enjoyment – only for information and instructions, for technology, food production and resource conservation. Ann recognises that she can 'survive' without novels – but the quality of her life will be poorer without the inspiration and pleasure they offer.

'If you'd lend me the suit...'

This is the first conflict between Ann and Loomis over the suit. Ann says 'That is what Edward had been up against'. Can you see the similarities between the two confrontations? (Look back at Chapter 11). Thinking further, what did Edward have to try, when Loomis refused to lend him the suit? Ann will be forced to do the same – not just to get books, but to preserve the life of freedom and humanity that they represent, and that Loomis tries to repress.

Survival

'You must plan. Not just for next year, but beyond.'

Loomis has started thinking about the future as if they are 'starting a colony, one that will last'. This is what Ann calls a 'long-term view' of survival. What does a 'colony' imply? Think about food supply – and population growth!

Loomis is the type of person who needs to have the future organised and under his control: a careful and rigid planner. We sense that food production is almost an obsession with him – perhaps because it is not something he knows about or can do himself (yet). He calls Ann 'foolish and short-sighted' for not thinking ahead. Do you agree with him? Ann says Loomis' vision of the future is 'nearly the same' as hers, but we are beginning to see the difference between his plans and her hopes.

John Loomis

Notice that Loomis even tells Ann, sarcastically, what to pray for. As with his scorn of novels, it is as if he is trying to belittle Ann's inner life – or even to make it part of his cold, practical plans.

Chapter 16

June 24th. *Loomis watches Ann work, and she grows uneasy. She realises he is still a stranger, and in the evening, she tries to get him to talk about himself. When she asks if he was ever married, he seems to take it as a hint that Ann is interested in him sexually. He grabs her hand and pulls her close, challenging her to admit it. The moment passes, but Ann is dismayed.*

Loomis watches Ann work

This is another mirror image of the days of Loomis' illness. Remember when

he watched her dig in Chapter 7. What is different about the way he watches now? Also, note his words to Ann: 'The important thing is not to let the species die out' ('the species' meaning the human race). What does this imply about his attitude to survival – and his intentions towards Ann?

Companionship

Who *is* John Loomis?

John Loomis

As Loomis was falling ill, Ann got to know him, but now that he is recovering, he seems more and more like a stranger: another mirror image. Ann says that at first, to her lonely eyes, Loomis 'had seemed attractive and friendly', but now it worries her that she knows so little about him. Consider Ann's theory about why he does not talk about the past: do you think she is right, or is Loomis just a rather cold and secretive person?

The 'pass'

Companionship

Why does Loomis think Ann is asking him if he is married? He has sensed (or just assumed) that Ann is 'interested' in him. Do you think he is teasing her (rather cruelly) for having an innocent crush on him? Or does he assume that she is not so innocent, and is sexually attracted to him? In which case, when he grabs her, is he just calling her bluff – or is he really trying to make a 'pass' at her? Since we only see Loomis from Ann's point of view, we cannot know for sure – as with most of his thoughts, we share Ann's frustration at how little we know.

Ann Burden

Either way, Loomis is heavy-handed, suggestive and cynical – in contrast to Ann's sensitivity and innocence. She is old-fashioned and inexperienced: she does not know how to handle a sexual advance – let alone such a threatening one – and has no parents to talk to about it. How can you tell that Ann is deeply upset by this? How does she handle it?

Loomis makes the hand-holding a mirror image of something that happened earlier: when he was ill, Ann held his hand. Ann says 'But it was not the same at all'. What is the difference? Consider Ann's motives in holding the sick man's hand.

> Ann senses that by making a pass at her, Loomis 'was just **taking charge, or possession**'. He tends to do this with everything: Ann identifies the planting, the petrol, the tractor and even her going to church. How has he 'taken charge' of these things?

Chapter 17

June 30th. *Another week has passed, and Ann is back in her cave: she explains what happened in her diary. The day after Loomis made the 'pass' at her, things seemed normal, but Ann was aware of him watching her as she worked in the fields. That evening, he asked her to read to him, as she did when he was ill.*

Time

Robert O'Brien uses the 'hook' technique again: what has happened to force Ann back to the cave? Having aroused our curiosity, Ann goes back to June 25th (the day after the 'pass') and picks up the story. She catches up with the events of June 30th itself at the end of Chapter 19.

'It was all as before except for my own feelings'

Ann Burden

Ann shows her resilience and courage on the morning after the 'pass'. Note how she goes about coping with her anxiety: work and nature usually make Ann feel better about things. Look carefully at the mentions of Loomis: how do they convey Ann's uneasiness about him?

Loomis asks Ann to read to him (again)

Loomis uses subtle psychological force to make Ann read, despite her reluctance. Like the hand-holding, Loomis uses the reading to remind Ann of her tenderness to him when he was ill (in Chapter 12): another mirror image. Then, it was a spontaneous gesture of hope and friendship: now, it seems 'strange and unnatural'. Loomis manages to spoil the memory, and even Ann's joy in books. Do you think he is doing this deliberately: another way of taking possession of Ann's inner life? Ann struggles to believe that he may really want to be read to. What do you think?

Pride and Prejudice, by Jane Austen, is about two people who dislike each other, having judged each other too hastily, but who eventually fall in love. Ann and Loomis seem to be going through the opposite process...

Chapter 18

June 30th (continued). *On the second evening, Loomis asks Ann to play the piano for him, but then deliberately tries to make her nervous. On the third evening, Ann finds him outside, checking on the safe-suit. She goes to bed uneasily, and in the night, Loomis tries to rape her. Alerted by Faro, she gets free and flees into the night.*

Loomis asks Ann to play the piano (again)

As with the reading, Loomis subtly uses Ann's piano-playing to intimidate

Companionship

her – without doing anything she can specifically object to. She played spontaneously for him when he was ill: first to give him pleasure (Chapter 7), then to will him to live (Chapter 12). Now, she plays anxiously and cannot finish even a hymn – her favourite music. Note how Loomis makes Ann even more aware of his presence than she already is. He may just be trying to frighten her, but this seems like a more sexual sort of taunt, like the hand-holding. Note what Loomis says to Ann before she goes to bed: why might it keep her awake?

Everything was quiet

Life and death

This is like the moment of calm before a storm. Small, natural details (especially sounds) make Ann's walk with Faro seem quiet, peaceful and hopeful. Note the baby crow which Ann saved, alive in its nest. What spoils the moment for Ann – and what details make the incident seem so sinister?

Loomis tries to rape Ann

Is this just a necessary step in Loomis' logical plans not to let the species die

Companionship

out? Or is he also gratifying his own sexual needs? Either way, he intends to use Ann ruthlessly for his own purposes, with no thought for her feelings at all. Note that at first, he touches her 'not roughly, but in a dreadful, possessive way': he wants to own and control her body, like everything else. The writing moves suddenly from breathless suspense to vivid, explosive action: how do you feel as you read it?

> Ann's leaving the house marks the end of the central phase of the novel. The phase has been shaped by the fall and rise of Loomis. Remember Ann's earliest fears of the stranger: has Loomis turned out to be 'crazy', 'mean', 'cruel', 'brutal', 'a murderer'? (Chapter 1). Has he tried to 'do whatever he likes' or make Ann a 'slave'? (Chapter 4).
>
> In the third phase, we are back with Ann hiding in the cave, afraid and suspicious of Loomis' intentions and of Faro's innocent betrayal. This is almost a mirror image of the first phase. But this time, Loomis is very much aware of Ann's presence: she is part of his plans – and Loomis, as we know, does not give up his plans without a fight...

Self-test (Questions) Chapters 14–18

Uncover the plot

Delete two of the three alternatives given, to find the correct plot. Beware possible misconceptions and muddles.

Loomis dies/recovers/worsens for Ann's fifteenth/sixteenth/seventeenth birthday. He seems worried about the suit/tractor/planting, and secretly works at driving/walking/ploughing. He wants literary/technical/poetry books, but forbids/allows/encourages Ann to borrow the suit/tractor/wagon to get food/water/novels. He starts to hope/plan/despair, as if they are 'starting a family/world/colony'. He helps/won't let/watches Ann work, like 'a spectator/a friend/an overseer'. She asks him about Edward/himself/Ithaca, and he grabs/rapes/

ignores her: Ann feels he is giving up/taking charge/going mad. The next night he asks her to read/play/cook for him: Ann is increasingly hopeful/uneasy/happy. One night, after Ann has been to the store/church/wagon, Loomis tries to rape/kiss/kill her.

Who? What? Why? When? Where? How?

1 Who has played the piano for Loomis before?
2 Who suggests that Ann could play the piano this time?
3 Why does Loomis want books?
4 What is Ann's explanation for Loomis' reluctance to talk about the past?
5 Where does Ann hope to get books from?
6 Where does Ann go on her walk, the evening of the attempted rape, and what does she notice?
7 Why has Ann not started planting, and what does Loomis think of her reasons?
8 Why does Loomis insist on growing beets and wheat?
9 How does Loomis make a pass at Ann?
10 How has Loomis begun to consider the valley, now that he is going to live?

Who said that?

From your knowledge of the characters in the book, identify the following speakers.

1 Who says: 'The important thing is not to let the species die out'?
2 Who says: 'I could survive without novels', and what is the important word here?
3 Who says: 'You must plan. Not just for next year, but beyond'?

Mirror images

What incident in Chapters 6–13 do the following 'mirror' and what is the difference now?

1 Ann cooks a special festive dinner, with candles (14)
2 Loomis thinks taking the suit to find novels is 'too foolish to consider' (15)
3 Loomis watches Ann working in the fields (16)
4 Loomis asks Ann to read to him (17)
5 Loomis asks Ann to play the piano for him (18)
6 Ann catches Loomis outside by the wagon (18)

Danger signs

These chapters end in Loomis' attempt to rape Ann. Have we suspected this would happen? Let's explore…

1 What two 'surprising things' does Loomis do in Chapter 14?
2 What causes (a) a 'rather tense silence' and (b) Ann's feeling 'uneasy' in Chapter 15?
3 What hints are there in Chapter 16 that Loomis is planning to have sex with Ann?
4 What is ominous about Loomis' behaviour in Chapter 17?

Who's in charge here?

When Loomis holds Ann's hand, she feels he is 'taking charge, or possession'. How has he done this with the other things she mentions: (a) the planting? (b) the use of the petrol? (c) the tractor? (d) Ann's going to church? (e) the suit? (f) Edward?

Chapter 19

June 30th (continued). *Ann flees to the store, then to the cave. She knows that Loomis will try to find her. In the morning, he watches Faro follow her tracks towards the store: fortunately, he cannot see where the dog goes from there. Ann does not feed Faro at the cave, so he returns to the house – and is tied up by Loomis. Ann thinks about the future and hopes that she and Loomis might be able to share the valley, while living apart.*

Ann is afraid

Ann Burden

Everything in the tale of Ann's flight helps to convey how shocked and scared she is, and heightens the sense of danger. We identify with Ann through very physical details, like her heartbeats and hard breathing. Can you find other physical symptoms of her fear?

Ann watches from the cave

As in the early chapters of the book, Ann is hiding in the cave, watching Loomis and trying to guess his intentions. But there is a big difference: Loomis knows that Ann is there, and is trying to find her – so Faro's return to Loomis is a much more immediate threat.

Faro is tied up

Note that Faro is used to freedom, and hates his captivity: Ann identifies with this completely, and will fight to stay free when Loomis tries to imprison her in turn (in Chapter 23).

Ann thinks the situation through

Ann is dutiful and considerate, wanting to keep up the farm work. It is

Survival
necessary for her own survival, but she also thinks about the welfare of the animals, and about Loomis (who is still too weak to fetch supplies). She cannot let him starve, whatever he has done. Ann thinks in terms of a compromise, so that they can share the valley, 'even though not as friends'. She sees – as Loomis cannot – that there is 'enough room' for both.
Note also that Ann wants to confront the problem openly, by talking to Loomis: look out for further examples of this in the following chapters.

When Ann says 'I woke up in the late afternoon...', we have finally arrived at June 30th, the day on which she started writing Chapter 17!

Chapter 20

June 31st. *Loomis has started training Faro to follow Ann's tracks on a leash. Ann goes to the house to confront him. He acts as if nothing has happened, and tells her*

she is childish not to return. He accepts her offer to tend the farm and feed him, in return for leaving her alone – but Ann suspects he is plotting to find her hiding place. The system seems to work for a day, but Loomis keeps training Faro and learns to drive the tractor. Ann begins to wish Loomis had never come to the valley, and wonders whether there are other places like it, perhaps nearby.

Loomis plans to use Faro to track Ann

Ann has worried about this since Faro first appeared: the threat is finally real. Robert O'Brien creates suspense by suggesting that, although Loomis is not yet strong enough to walk as far as the cave, it is only a matter of time.

A game of chess

Hope

Ann realises that she is in a battle of wits with Loomis: each has to outguess and outmanoeuvre the other, as in a game of chess. Ann feels hopelessly that only Loomis can win – but she also turns out to be good at the 'game'. Note how clear she is at avoiding, and setting, traps in the following chapters.

'I took stock of what I had in the cave'

Survival

Ann is back to providing for basic survival needs: see how she plans for food, clothes, water, fire and protection. We hear about such things much more often, now that Ann is again forced to live by her wits. If you keep a diary, do you ever put down what you have for meals? Why might such things be more important in Ann's situation?

'I thought you would come back,' he said. '...I hoped you would.'

When Loomis says 'Not come back? But why not?', Ann realises that he is

John Loomis

not sorry at all for what he has done. (The reason 'why not' is that he tried to rape her!) Is Loomis is trying to pretend that the incident never happened, to avoid feeling guilty? Or is he so selfish and cynical that he really does not see it as any big deal? He thinks Ann is 'acting like a schoolgirl' (presumably he means over-sensitive and silly) by insisting on living apart.

Meanwhile, notice his subtle attempts to find out where she stays at night.

> **Faro** has become a jealously-guarded part of Loomis' plans, like the suit. Ann realises that Loomis fears she will 'steal' the dog, as Edward stole the suit. She is also part of his plans: she recognises that Loomis plans to imprison her too.

'I put it out of my mind and milked the cow'

Farm work, as usual, makes Ann feel more hopeful, even happy. She is absolutely fair in dividing the produce and still thinks of 'sharing' the valley.

Her confidence is spoiled, however, by Loomis' plotting. He now learns to drive the tractor: we shall soon find out why.

'I wish now Mr Loomis had never come to the valley at all'

Companionship

Loomis had earlier predicted that Ann would feel this way. Ann herself guessed that 'there are worse things than being alone', and now she knows it. She wishes that Loomis had found some other valley – which leads her to consider the possibility that other places might have survived the war.

Chapter 21

August 4th (Ann thinks). *Ann is hiding in the hills, having been shot by Loomis. For ten days after her last diary entry, Ann worked and took Loomis his share of the food, and he left her alone. Meanwhile, Loomis was getting stronger, training Faro, practising in the tractor, and spying on Ann: she took a roundabout route to and from the cave. One day, Loomis would not let Ann use the tractor: she realised that it was another thing he had taken over.*

'Mr Loomis *shot* me. I haven't written in my diary for several weeks.'

Time

This is the most striking 'hook' in the novel: we have to wait until Chapter 23 to find out what happened. It is also the beginning of a complex time sequence. Ann is now unsure of the exact date (her calendar is in the house), but it is over a month since her last entry. The events from July 1st to August 4th are told in Chapters 21–23 (written on August 4th) and Chapter 24 (written on August 6th). The length of this five-week flashback allows Ann, for the first time, the benefit of hindsight. She drops hints about things that happen later, arousing our curiosity: look out for examples.

'For about ten days we had a sort of system.'

Ann has established a routine of working and supplying Loomis, but the situation is uneasy. Loomis is making progress with his walking, Faro's training and the tractor (for reasons we find out in the next chapter).

On the morning of the tenth day...

Hope

Loomis is spying on the road to see Ann arrive: Ann outwits him by going round and appearing near the store. Notice that her route takes her past the crab-apple tree: it is no longer flowering, but bearing the early signs of bitter fruit. What does this say about Ann and Loomis?

'There was an obvious solution to both problems'

Note how Ann leaves the pond and reappears a few minutes later, having fetched her knife and milk pail from the cave. She thinks she has escaped suspicion, but writing with hindsight, she admits: 'As it turned out, I was wrong'. We find out how in a moment...

'And then my serious trouble began'

Loomis has taken the keys to the tractor. Ann guesses that he wants to 'ration' the tractor's use to save petrol: this would be fairly typical of him. (Again, with hindsight she hints that she was wrong about this: it keeps us guessing.) Note how open and honest Ann is, in going to Loomis to ask for the key.

'Back again?', he said, very pleasant.

Loomis is friendly on the surface, at first, but there are nasty undercurrents.

John Loomis

See how he hints that: (a) he knows Ann has been watching him; (b) he controls things, and can make Ann's life difficult if she stays away; (c) he is independent of her now; and (d) he has been watching her. Note the even more subtle hint that he knows she lives close to the pond: he had noticed her quick return with the knife and milk pail, earlier.

The truth about the tractor

Ann realises that Loomis has taken the key to keep the tractor for himself: to stop her 'stealing' it from him, like the safe-suit and Faro. Like them, it has become part of his plans, and is therefore to be under his total, jealous control.

> The **tractor** is a symbol of survival attitudes. Ann has used it joyfully to grow crops they can both share. Loomis uses it to control the food supply in the valley, and for speed in pursuing Ann (see Chapter 22).

Chapter 22

August 4th (continued). *Ann was near the store when she heard the tractor coming. Hiding, she watched Loomis 'storm' the store, gun in hand: he thought Ann was living there, in the Kleins' apartment. On leaving, he padlocked the doors. Ann feared he might not let her get supplies from there again.*

Loomis on the warpath

This explains all the hints about the tractor: Loomis uses its speed to chase Ann. He thinks she is living above the store, because he saw her appear near it (in the previous chapter). Loomis' cautious behaviour is sinister, but also comic: he looks to Ann like an Indian attacking a wagon train in an old Western.

The Kleins' apartment

Ann's description is full of gentle sadness. Note the details that make the scene both intensely private and bleakly empty. What is the effect of hinting that the last thing the Kleins did was to look at the photograph?

'I thought of the gun again'

Ann thought at first that Loomis was carrying a gun because he meant to shoot her. Now, she feels that he is just being cautious, fearing that *she* might shoot *him*. Ann traces his thought processes: they say a lot about Loomis' methodical thinking – but also about Ann's.

Ann has got used to the way Loomis' mind worked, and has noticed a 'pattern' in Loomis' behaviour. In Chapter 21, the tractor, safe-suit and Faro were 'part of a pattern' of obsessive planning, fear and mistrust. Can you see the same pattern in his carrying a gun? The patterns all seem to reflect what happened in the laboratory with Edward.

Loomis locks the store

Can you see how locking the store might be part of the same pattern as his behaviour over Faro, the tractor and the suit?

Chapter 23

August 4th (continued). *The following morning, Ann decided to ask Loomis about the store. At the house, Loomis shot her in the ankle, intending to cripple and capture her. She managed to run to the cave, but Loomis came after her, using Faro to follow her trail. Ann realised she would have to shoot Faro to avoid being caught, but at the last moment, could not do it. Loomis destroyed her cave camp.*

Ann confronts Loomis about the store

Like the tractor and the gun, there are two ways of looking at Loomis' locking

of the store. Perhaps he did not trust Ann to ration the provisions properly. (Ann recognises his 'compulsion for taking charge of things, for saving things, for rationing them out in an orderly manner'. Can you think of examples?) The other alternative (which Ann later accepts) is that he is trying to starve her into going back to him.

Ann again decides to be open with Loomis, and even to be friendly: maybe he is desperate for her return because he 'cannot stand being alone'. (A possibility, as we shall see in the final chapter.) Her generosity makes what happens next all the more pointless and shocking. Note how Robert O'Brien slowly works up to the shooting, to increase the suspense. The shooting itself is an explosion of sound and movement.

Loomis shoots to maim

When Ann stops to wonder why Loomis did not kill her, she realises that he

Time

deliberately wounded her to capture her. The idea of being his prisoner horrifies Ann. What follows is like a nightmare to her. As she writes about it (weeks later) she relives it again – so the passage is written in the present tense ('I am sitting…') This makes the events seem much more immediate, and we identify closely with Ann.

Faro or Ann?

Survival

Note how Ann's description makes Faro seem a loveable, friendly dog. This makes it more horrible that Loomis has turned him into an enemy – and that Ann will have to shoot him to protect herself. She is quite calm and deliberate – but she cannot do it. What changes her mind? Look at the words she uses to describe Faro's bark.

> Ann has now faced the **kill-or-be-killed dilemma**, as Loomis did with Edward. Unlike Loomis, she could not kill to protect herself. To Ann, life is precious: she will even feel the same way with Loomis at the very end of the book. The mere fact that she *meant* to kill Faro makes Ann feel 'as much a murderer as Mr Loomis'. Do you agree with this view, or do you think her moral honesty sets her apart from Loomis?

Loomis destroys Ann's camp

Ann's survival skills will now be put to an extreme test. Consider what she

Art and science

managed to salvage: could you survive a month in the wilderness with only these items? Note that Ann's last book was burned: a symbol of Loomis' destruction of Ann's life in the valley.

Ann comes out of the flashback, to comment on the story she has just told. She also tells us something that happens later: she does kill Faro, though not with a gun. How does this statement make you feel?

Chapter 24

August 6th. *Ann continues the 'flashback'. After she was shot, she became feverish. She had a recurring dream about a place outside the valley, and decided to try and find* *it – by stealing the safe-suit. For almost a month, she lived rough, while Loomis ignored her and worked the land. She hesitated to put her plan in motion, until one day Loomis left the store open: a trap for her. Alerted at the last moment, Ann escaped and was hunted by Loomis, with Faro. She ambushed him and fired a shot over his head: he fled, but Faro came on – across the poisoned Burden Creek. He died the next day.*

Back in the present, Ann is about to put her plan into action.

Time

Writing now in the present, Ann drops the bombshell that she is going to steal the safe-suit and leave the valley. She then picks up the story where she left off, to explain how she got the idea. This chapter continues the events of the four-week gap in Ann's diary, before she picked it up again on August 4th.

A feverish dream

Dreams

Loomis had guilty nightmares, but Ann has a recurring dream containing all her hopes: a living valley, books, children, teaching. Do you think she is dreaming about this because she wants it so much, or is there such a place which Ann is somehow seeing? Ann first 'hopes', then 'believes', it is true.

'And so I decided to leave the valley.'

Life and death

John Loomis

The valley has been home and shelter to Ann all her life: now it is threatening. Note how even small natural sounds – usually a source of peace to her – have become frightening. The 'poison' is Loomis.

Ann has given up hope of living in peace with Loomis, because she now believes he is 'insane'. Consider his intense manner, his obsessive behaviour and sudden mood swings. Perhaps he really is mentally unstable, after the trauma of the laboratory and the deadness: the guilt, fear and loneliness. Does this excuse his behaviour to Ann?

Ann decides to look for the place she has seen in her dream. We have been prepared for the possibility of other living valleys (look back at Chapter 20). It does not seem unrealistic for Ann to hope: she is a dreamer, but also a practical thinker.

'Yet for almost a month he has left me alone.'

Art and science

As Ann develops her plans, weeks pass by. Loomis is busy in the fields. (She wonders if he is trying to trick her: as we will see, he does have a plan.) Ann leads a miserable life in the hills: afraid, hungry and worst of all, bored. Note that it is the thought of her last book (which Loomis burned) that finally stirs her 'hardest feelings' towards him. It was not just the book, but Loomis' malice: by burning it, he 'deliberately ruined the thing I prized most'. Stealing the safe-suit will be a fitting revenge.

Ann hesitates: Loomis acts

Unusually for her, Ann drifts without taking action: she is afraid of Loomis (who has already killed for the suit once) and lulled by the seeming truce. Loomis breaks the deadlock by setting a trap for Ann at the store.

The death of Faro

Ann boldly ambushes Loomis from across Burden Creek, scaring him off with a shot from the gun he was not sure she had. In Chapter 25, Ann says she was 'setting a trap for Faro': she deliberately hid where he would follow her across the creek. She has killed him after all. This is the last straw for Ann: sad and angry, she takes action at last.

Hope

Ann ends the flashback which began in Chapter 21. It is August 6th, the night before she tries to steal the safe-suit. This is a sombre moment: if her plan fails, she will not live to write her diary again. She poignantly recalls the ploughing (in Chapter 9), and her joyful hopes of a future with Loomis. Her expectations of him are now very different...

Chapter 25

August 7th. *Ann, wearing the safe-suit, is waiting to confront Loomis. Before dawn, she had left a note, asking him to meet her at the south end of the valley. He fell for it. Ann got to the suit and wagon, and, full of fear and regrets, set off. She feels she has to speak to Loomis one last time, though he will probably say and do anything to stop her leaving – even kill her. Ann finishes writing: Loomis is on his way.*

Time crowds in, as Ann writes up just a few hours' events. We know immediately that she has successfully got the safe-suit, but Robert O'Brien keeps the tension high, by leaving Ann to wait for Loomis: the story of her escape is told under the shadow of his approach and the threat of violence.

Ann waits for Loomis

Ann Burden

Ann shows her openness – and great emotional courage – in refusing to leave without seeing Loomis again. She is afraid and vulnerable, yet determined. She is desperate, yet still humane: she knows she could not kill Loomis, even to save herself.

The night before

Ann weighs up the risks. Note the echo of the 'chess game' which, earlier, it seemed only Loomis could win. In real chess, Ann used to beat her more skilled father by going on the attack, putting him on the defensive: she has done this to Loomis at the creek. Amidst the planning, note how Ann is aware of the strange beauty of the night: it makes her feel as if she is already on a journey. Moments of mysterious stillness alternate with bursts of action: see how Ann watches the sunrise, after delivering the note. These moments help us to sense the enormity of the step Ann is about to take into the unknown.

The plan

Ann's note (our first clue to her plan) is very cleverly written. It suggests willingness to surrender and calms Loomis' fears of being shot at, while showing believable caution about *his* going armed.

Ann heads for the deadness

As Ann pulls the wagon away, time seems to slow down. Her mind fills with bits of childhood memories and discarded hopes. She is intensely aware of sounds, sights, sensations. Every step away from the valley makes her realise how precious it is to her. See how fear and sadness deaden her hopes: she can hardly see the children of her dream any more. When she thinks of Loomis'

Hope

desperate arguments, it is as if she is wearing down her own hope and courage with the 'horrors of the deadness'.

> Ann passes **Burden Creek**: it is clear and beautiful to her – but it kills everything it touches. How might this echo her feelings about **Loomis**?

Ann somehow finds the courage to face Loomis at the top of Burden Hill. What would you want to say to him, if you were Ann?

Chapter 26

August 8th. *Loomis arrives, enraged. Despite her fear, Ann cannot shoot him. At the sound of her voice, he fires towards her hiding place: Ann reveals herself, accepting that she is going to die. Loomis wildly demands the safe-suit. Ann refuses, saying he can kill her, as he killed Edward. At the mention of Edward's name, Loomis seems to cave in. Ann tells him that his own selfish, controlling behaviour has forced her to take the suit. He begs her not to leave him alone. She walks out into the deadness – and Loomis does not shoot her. He shouts that he had seen birds circling in the west (a sign of life). Ann goes on her way – with hope.*

'...the way you killed Edward.'

We cannot know why these words should stop Loomis in his tracks. Sheer

John Loomis

surprise that Ann knew? Shame, because Ann had nursed and befriended him when she knew he was a murderer? Guilt about Edward – perhaps faced for the first time? The realisation that he was repeating his nightmare with Ann? In any case, his body and voice betray his confusion.

Ann forces Loomis to face up to the consequences of his selfish and tyrannical behaviour: her words have real dignity and moral power. Loomis breaks down, bewildered and afraid, begging not to be left alone. Ann never thought he was evil, only 'insane'. Here, we see him for the weak and damaged person that he is. Do you feel sorry for him?

Companionship

Ann is bitter about the tractor, the store and the valley – but not just because they were hers. They are all things for which Loomis fought Ann, when she only wanted to share them with him: symbols of his rejection, insensitivity and ingratitude, and the ruin of all her hopes of a future with him. Ann's final words *do* sound childish, as her self-control cracks – but they arise from the same real sense of hurt and disappointment.

'That was all'

Perhaps Loomis wants to show his gratitude after all – his last impulse is

John Loomis

generous. Note that he calls Ann by name: he has only done that once before, in Chapter 10. We leave Loomis safe, secure and in control, as he wanted – but having lost his only friend: the story of the laboratory, and the story of the valley. Do you feel the same sense of hope for Loomis as for Ann, as the book ends? Will he become a contented, balanced human being, left to himself in the valley?

> **Birds** are a literal sign of life for Ann to follow: remember, birds do not survive in the deadness, so circling birds suggest a living valley. They are also symbols of hope to Ann.

Now it is morning

Hope

Despite the bleak deadness, Ann's hope has returned. Whether the place in her dream is real or imaginary, the signs are good. She dreams again, this time of actually finding her schoolroom. The birds, the stream and the sun all lead her westward. She has purpose and direction. The book ends on the words: 'I am hopeful'.

Self-test (Questions) Chapters 19–26

Uncover the plot
Delete two of the three alternatives given, to find the correct plot. Beware possible misconceptions and muddles.

Ann stays in the store/church/cave, planning to leave/work/burn the farm and shoot/feed/ starve Loomis. He kills/captures/frees Faro and tries to find Ann's guns/hideout/keys. He takes the keys to the store/tractor/church, fearing Ann will use/steal/waste it. Then he storms the cave/church/store and burns/locks/ opens it. When Ann asks/prowls/lies about it, he shoots to kill/maim/miss her: in the ensuing hunt, she decides/tries/wants to kill Faro. Ann dreams of a house/ school/church and decides to leave the cave/valley/hills. Loomis traps Ann at the Creek/house/store, but Ann runs Faro/Loomis/herself into Burden Creek. Ann destroys/leaves/ steals the suit and goes – before/without/after seeing Loomis. The word 'think/Edward/kill' makes him raise/drop/fire his gun. As Ann leaves, he points towards green/birds/streams.

Who? What? Why? When? Where? How?
1 Who says: 'Don't leave me. Don't leave me here alone'?
2 What is Ann's plan for Loomis and herself to share the valley?
3 What is Ann's plan to steal the suit?
4 What is the stealing of the suit Ann's 'revenge' for?
5 Where does Loomis think Ann is living and why?
6 Where does Ann wait for her final confrontation with Loomis?
7 Why does Loomis not shoot to kill Ann (a) in Chapter 23 and (b) in Chapter 26?
8 Why does Ann decide to leave the valley, and what makes her finally do it?
9 How has Loomis deduced that Ann has a gun – and when is he sure?
10 How does Ann kill Faro?

Mirror images
What other event or situation does each of the following reflect, and what is the difference?
1 Ann is hiding in the cave, secretly watching Loomis
2 Ann does not feed Faro at the cave, so he returns to Loomis
3 Ann decides to shoot Faro to protect herself, and feels like a murderer
4 Ann 'cannot let (Loomis) starve', and 'could not kill' him

Part of a pattern?
What past or future behaviour by Loomis does Ann feel is suggested by the following?
1 Loomis acts as if the attempted rape never happened (20)
2 Loomis catches Faro and keeps him prisoner, intending to train him to be obedient (19)
3 Loomis keeps Faro away from Ann, in case she 'steals' him (20)
4 Loomis takes the keys to the tractor and the store: (two possible 'patterns') (21, 23)
5 Loomis takes his gun when he goes after Ann at the store (22)

Familiar themes
Many of the major themes come together in the last chapter of the book. Let's explore…
1 What does Ann dream, and how is it different from before?
2 What sentence sums up Ann's outlook as she heads west?

3   What symbols of life and death are mentioned as Ann heads into the deadness?
4   What struggles to survive are recalled during Ann's last confrontation with Loomis?
5   What features of the valley are we reminded of?
6   How, according to Ann, has Loomis treated her – and why is this ironic?
7   What do you notice about how Ann and Loomis are left to survive?

Last word on revision

Mnemonics are word games that help you remember lists of things. Here are some do-it-yourself examples, that might be helpful. Take the word CROPS. Think of all the words beginning with 'C' that you associate with Ann: now do the same with the other letters. CROPS also works quite well for Loomis' characteristics: have a go.

Self-test (Answers) Chapters 1–5

Uncover the plot

Ann lives in Burden Valley. There has been a war. Ann's family and the Kleins have died, but the valley is green. Then Ann sees smoke, and feels 'both excited and afraid'. A stranger arrives in a 'plastic-looking ' suit, and Ann decides to watch him. From her cave, she sees him explore the farm. He even shoots a chicken. He finds minnows in the pond, and jumps into Burden Creek. Next day, he walks south towards the gap, where the streams join. Returning, he becomes ill. Ann wants him to live, and goes to the tent to help. The man says: 'Edward'. He has radiation poisoning.

Who? What? Why? When? Where? How?

1   Ann's – but only that her surname is Burden (2)
2   Ann's cousin, Ann's brother, David's dog, the store owners (1, 2)
3   She lets the animals run wild, digs up the garden, takes the flowers from the church (2)
4   Go to Teachers' College and become an English teacher (1)
5   The north end and south end of the valley (4)
6   To keep track; companionship. Something really important: the smoke (1)
7   The family/Kleins: to check on the Amish. Joseph: not to be left behind (1)
8   He is hot; has not bathed for ages. He thinks it is the one from the pond; does not check (3)
9   Clear one: fish, plants etc. Poisoned one: no life, dead things, dead grass beside it (2, 4)
10 It is closed in by hills: winds and weather from outside do not enter (4)

Who's who?

1   Ann (1). Loomis (3)
2   Ann and Loomis. Loomis (3)
3   Faro (3)
4   Ann (4)

Natural science

1   She grows vegetables, keeps animals, gets water from the stream, chops wood for fire (2)
2   Electricity – for furnace and pump: problem of warmth and water supply. Gas stove (when gas ran out): problem of cooking. Radio: problem of checking time/date (2)
3   Radiation-proof suit, airtank (2), tent and supply wagon, Geiger counters (3)
4   Nuclear bombs, nerve gas, chemical and other weapons (3). Also medical techniques (5)

I want to be alone

1   She hated it; longed for anyone to come. The radio hinted at selfish and brutal behaviour (1)
2   Crazy; mean; cruel; brutal; murderer (1)
3   Someone to talk to, work with, plan for the future. A man – so she can have a family (4)
4   He is ill. She dreams of her family and realises she cannot bear to be alone again (5)
5   He cheers (3); looks 'poetic', 'almost handsome' and 'quite nice' (2–4). He is friendly to Faro (4)

War game

1 Telephones going dead (1). Radio stations telling about it, then going dead (1). Death of people and birds in Ogdentown (1). Deadness all around (1)
2 Widespread death suggests radiation, ie nuclear bombs (1). As do radioactive cars (1) and Geiger counters (3). The war lasted only a week (2). Nerve gas, bacteria etc were used (3)
3 Nothing moving (1). No birds returned (3). Burden Creek still poisoned (2, 3). Loomis in suit (2)
4 Ann's family: concern for friends (1). People fighting for food on radio ship (1). Ann and Loomis cautious, even suspicious (1, 3). Hint at shooting of Edward (5)

Self-test (Answers) Chapters 6–13

Uncover the plot

The stranger's name is John Loomis. He was a chemist at Cornell University, working on a radiation-proof plastic called polapoly with Professor Kylmer when the war began. Ann works the farm and Loomis suggests getting petrol. Ann notices a crab-apple tree in bloom, and thinks of marrying Loomis. She gets the tractor going and ploughs happily – but Loomis is suddenly worse. He dreams about Edward. Ann discovers that in the laboratory, Loomis shot Edward to keep the suit for himself. Ann prays that Loomis will live.

Who? What? Why? When? Where? How?

1 Edward's wife and son (11)
2 A Nobel-prize-winning chemist, Loomis' head of department and then boss (6)
3 Ann's piano-playing gives him 'the best evening of his life' (7) He longs to go fishing (8)
4 Ann's dream of her mother (8). Loomis' nightmares about Edward (10, 11)
5 Ann's Bible Letter book. She thought Zachariah was the last man – like Loomis (7)
6 In the church, with a proper ceremony and apple blossom (8)
7 So its troops could live (and fight) on during a nuclear war (6)
8 It combines helping people with reading and books (13)
9 People had killed each other to get into the shelter, and destroyed its air supply (6)
10 Ann rejoices and wants to share her triumph. Loomis is 'matter-of-fact' (9)

Who said that?

1 Ann (7)
2 Loomis (9)
3 Ann (13)
4 Loomis (6)
5 Ann (12)

All about Edward

1 To find his family, in case they had survived outside, or at least to be sure (10, 11)
2 It was certain that Edward's family were dead (10, 11)
3 The suit was the 'last useful thing'; too important to risk, if something went wrong (10, 11)

4   Survival. The lab's air would run out: only the one with the suit could go out and live (10)
5   Take the suit while Loomis was asleep (10)

Clashing symbols
1   Ann's hopes of marriage to Loomis (8), gradually fading (12)
2   Power to survive, create life you want (Loomis: survival. Ann: books). The power of science: both positive (Ann/books) and destructive (Loomis/Edward)
3   Hope, new life, the importance of compassion (12)
4   Ann's sense of purpose, fulfilment in simple achievements (13)
5   The difference between Loomis' technical mind (8) and Ann's imagination (13)

In two minds
1   Choose from: calling valley 'theoretical possibility' (6), polapoly project (6), suggesting petrol for tractor (7), planning electricity generator (8), interest in technical books (8), teaching Ann to work petrol pump (9)
2   Choose from: playing piano (7), remembering Sunday School (7), reciting poem (9), praying for Loomis (11), reading Bible (11), reading and playing to Loomis (12), loves books/reading (13)
3   They try to share them, to help each other. Loomis gives knowledge, as he is too weak yet to help in other ways. Ann tries to give Loomis pleasure, hope and life

Self-test (Answers) Chapters 14–18

Uncover the plot
Loomis recovers for Ann's sixteenth birthday. He seems worried about the planting, and secretly works at walking. He wants technical books, but forbids Ann to borrow the suit to get novels. He starts to plan, as if they are 'starting a colony'. He watches Ann work, like 'an overseer'. She asks him about himself, and he grabs her: Ann feels he is taking charge. The next night he asks her to read for him: Ann is increasingly uneasy. One night, after Ann has been to the church, Loomis tries to rape her.

Who? What? Why? When? Where? How?
1   His cousin in Nyack, New York (16)
2   Loomis himself (18)
3   Technical information to help him design the electricity generator (15)
4   He hates to think about Edward, the lonely time in the lab, the walk in the deadness (16)
5   Ogdentown Library (15)
6   The church and the pond. The baby crow, first fireflies, fish: signs of life and hope (18)
7   She had to care for Loomis; went to church to pray for him. A waste of time (14)
8   For sugar and flour: basic supplies that will run out at the store (15)
9   He grabs her hand, pulls her close, challenges her to admit she is 'interested' in him (16)
10 As his, as well as Ann's (14)

Who said that?

1 Loomis (16)
2 Ann (15) – 'survive' (as opposed to 'enjoy life')
3 Loomis (15)

Mirror images

1 'Festive' fish and salad, the first evening of Loomis weakness (8) Ann does not see a difference, but we have seen signs of Loomis' growing strength
2 He thought this about Edward's hope of finding his family (10). No difference
3 He watched Ann dig the garden (7). Then, admiring her work: now, 'like an overseer'
4 She read to him (same 'Elegy') when he was unconscious (12). Now, he 'makes' her do it
5 She played to entertain him (7) and give him life (12). Now, she is reluctant and nervous
6 He went out to check the suit in delirium (10) Now, he is 'purposeful', and stronger

Danger signs

1 He scolds Ann about the delay in the planting and tries to get out of bed
2 (a) Loomis' anger at Ann's proposal to borrow suit; (b) Loomis' cold planning for the future
3 He does not want 'to let the species die out'. He makes a 'pass' at her
4 He acts as if nothing has happened; watches Ann; no longer stays in bed; makes Ann read

Who's in charge here?

(a) He hurries Ann, asks questions (14); tells her what to grow (15); watches her (16).
(b) He thought of it (7); makes her aware petrol won't last; cattle will have to pull plough (15)
(c) He makes tractor part of plans for self-sufficiency; tells Ann what to do with it (15)
(d) He tells her it was a waste of time (14); tells her what to pray for: his plans (15)
(e) Killed Edward for it (10,11); forbids Ann to touch it (15)
(f) Killed him (10, 11)

Self-test (Answers) Chapters 19–26

Uncover the plot

Ann stays in the cave, planning to work the farm and feed Loomis. He captures Faro and tries to find Ann's hideout. He takes the keys to the tractor, fearing Ann will steal it. Then he storms the store and locks it. When Ann asks about it, he shoots to maim her: in the ensuing hunt, she decides to kill Faro. Ann dreams of a school and decides to leave the valley. Loomis traps Ann at the store, but Ann runs Faro into Burden Creek. Ann steals the suit and goes – after seeing Loomis. The word 'Edward' makes him drop his gun. As Ann leaves, he points towards birds.

Who? What? Why? When? Where? How?

1 Loomis (26)
2 She will work the farm, feed Loomis, but live apart, perhaps in the store or church (19)

3 A note inviting Loomis to meet her at the gap. While he is gone, take the suit (25)
4 Loomis burning her last book, the thing she valued most (24)
5 The Kleins' apartment in the store: she seemed to come from there when he watched (22)
6 At the top of Burden Hill, on the edge of the deadness (25)
7 (a) He only wants to capture her. (b) She mentioned Edward
8 The valley is a threat; Loomis is insane; she dreams of somewhere else. Faro's death (24)
9 Farmers always have guns, but there were none in the house. The ambush at the creek (24)
10 She hides across Burden Creek, where Loomis and Faro will suddenly run into it (24)

Mirror images
1 As in Chapter 3–5, but now he knows she is there
2 As in Chapter 4, but now Faro will really be used to track Ann down (22)
3 Loomis 'murdered' Edward in self-defence. (11) Ann finds she cannot kill (23)
4 Loomis tries to starve Ann (23) and threatens to kill her (26)

Part of a pattern?
1 He pretended the 'pass' never happened, too (17) – as with the shooting of Edward?
2 He will try to do the same by maiming Ann (23)
3 He feared Edward would steal the suit (11)
4 (a) He has always been compulsive about 'saving' things. (b) He has guarded the suit and Faro from Ann in the same way, for his own purposes (in this case, trapping Ann)
5 He used a gun for protection on entering the valley (3) and with Edward (11): suspicion, fear

Familiar themes
1 Of a schoolroom, with children and books: this time, she actually finds them
2 'I am hopeful'
3 Life: birds, green, children. Death: deadness, brown grass
4 Ann's struggle against starvation and hunting by Loomis; Loomis' struggle against Edward and against illness. Set against easier survival in the valley
5 Deadness all around it. Inside food, and shelter
6 He has starved her, deprived her, hunted her, tried to imprison her, been ungrateful. Loomis needs her, and hates to be alone – but has driven her away
7 Loomis has the tractor, store and valley, ie nature. Ann has suit and wagon, ie science

Last word on revision (suggestions only)

Ann	Loomis
Caring, courageous, competent, clever, companionable, compassionate, cautious	Cunning, cold, calculating, competitive, cruel, controlling, clever, cautious
Resourceful, reading, religious	Ruthless, resourceful
Open, optimistic, old-fashioned	Obsessive, overbearing
Practical, positive, prayer, piano	Plans, power, possessive, pretence, paranoid
Spiritual, self-contained, sensitive, self-controlled, survivor, sharing	Selfish, survival, science